Giving Back

Giving Back
Connecting You, Business, and Community

BERT BERKLEY
Chairman, Tension Envelope Corporation

PETER ECONOMY
Associate Editor, *Leader to Leader*

WILEY

John Wiley & Sons. Inc.

For general information on our other products and services, or technical support, please contact our Customer Care Department within the United States at 800-762-2974, outside the United States at 317-572-3993 or fax 317-572-4002.

Wiley also publishes its books in a variety of electronic formats. Some content that appears in print may not be available in electronic books.

For more information about Wiley products, visit our Web site at http://www.wiley.com.

Library of Congress Cataloging-in-Publication Data:

Berkley, Bert.
　　Giving back : connecting you, business, and community / Bert Berkley, Peter Economy.
　　　　p.　cm.
　　Includes index.
　　ISBN 978-0-470-16753-3 (cloth)
　　　　1. Social action—United States—Case studies.　2. Community organization—United States—Case studies.　3. Voluntarism—United States—Case studies.　4. Social responsibility of business—United States—Case studies.　I. Economy, Peter.　II. Title.
　　HN65.B46　2008
　　361.7′650973—dc22

　　　　　　　　　　　　　　　　　　　　　　　　　　　　　　　　　　　　　　2007043560

Printed in the United States of America

10 9 8 7 6 5 4 3 2 1

This book is dedicated to the many millions of Americans who aren't just talking about society's problems, but who are doing something to solve them.

Contents

Foreword

BY HARVEY MACKAY

AUTHOR OF THE NEW YORK TIMES BEST SELLER, SWIM WITH THE SHARKS WITHOUT BEING EATEN ALIVE. NATIONALLY SYNDICATED COLUMNIST

You might think that by now, all of our social ills would be cured—that everyone in our great nation would have a home to live in, plenty of food to eat, access to adequate health care, steady and productive work, and lives free of discrimination and bias. After all, we are the wealthiest and most powerful nation in the history of the world, and our economic system is both a remarkably productive money-making machine and a shining beacon of hope to millions of people around the globe.

Nothing could be further from the truth. Take a moment to look around, and you'll quickly see that there remains much work to be done—homeless men, women, and children live on the street in cities across the country, children go to bed hungry at night, educational opportunities are lacking in many underserved neighborhoods. According to Centers for Disease Control and Prevention statistics, as of 2006, 43.3 million Americans under the age of 65 lacked health insurance coverage. And, according to the U.S. Census Bureau, as of 2006, 36.5 million Americans lived in poverty.

Long story short, there is a significant gap between the haves and the have-nots in our nation. This gap is closing very slowly, if at all.

While some believe government can and should provide all the answers to societal problems such as these, it's clear that government can't do it alone. There are just too many problems, and federal, state, and local governments—with their increasingly limited resources—are only able to do so much. Understanding this quandary, businesspeople have long stepped in to bridge the gap between what government can and cannot do—giving generously of their time, expertise, company resources, and networks of connections. Most of my own business and industry colleagues are very active in their communities, whether it's being involved in United Way campaigns, making donations to children's hospitals or trauma centers, volunteering for organizations such as Habitat for Humanity or scouting programs, or participating in the charitable activities of their churches or synagogues.

But what if you want to do more than simply write a check? What if you would like to create a lasting legacy that will enlist others to your cause and live on beyond you? In this book, Bert Berkley and Peter Economy provide businesspeople who want to give back—people like you—with an easy-to-follow blueprint for making a real difference in the world around them. Truth be told, you don't have to be a Bill Gates or a Warren Buffett to change the world. And you don't need to be CEO or chairman of the board. You just need to be able to identify a problem that needs to be solved, and have a commitment for solving it. Using numerous real-life case examples, Bert and Peter show that there are many different ways to give back, and that anyone can do it—on his or her own terms.

People who do volunteer work and help other people on a regular basis have a healthier outlook on life. They are more inclined to be go-getters and consistently report being happier. Young, old, professional, student, teacher, it doesn't matter. There's a great-unpaid job waiting for you. Did I say unpaid? Well, don't confuse that with unrewarding. In my own experience, I've consistently found that I get more than I give.

Find a cause that means something to you—education, politics, arts, environment, community service, religion—it doesn't matter. Organizations need help at every level.

I subscribe to the theory that 20 percent of your time should be devoted to volunteering. Sounds like a lot, until you find a cause that you can get passionate about. Then, there will never be enough time.

I am personally inspired by the examples in this book, and I hope you will be, too. As I am fond of saying, the boat won't go if we all don't row. Our nation needs your solutions, your hard work, and your commitment now more than ever before.

Acknowledgments

We would like to thank the individuals who graciously agreed to be interviewed for this book, including Roger Brown, S. Truett Cathy, Matt Flannery, Gary Hirshberg, Linda Mason, and Oz Nelson. We would also like to thank Marty Blank, Phyllis Brunson, Candace Cheatem, Frank Farrow, Gayle Hobbs, Harold Richman, Landon Rowland, Brent Schondelmeyer, Ralph Smith, and Gary Stangler for their guidance and contributions to this project. Finally, we would like to thank our editor at Wiley—Susan McDermott—for believing in this project and for her patience as we worked hard to meet our delivery dates.

In addition, Bert would like to thank his wife, Joan, who developed the idea that this book should be about several worthwhile projects across the country that encourage businesspeople to set an example with the hope that others will follow. Bert is indebted to his coauthor, who is a joy to work with and a superb craftsman.

And Peter would like to thank his coauthor Bert Berkley for sharing his vast wealth of knowledge and expertise in the fine art of giving back, and for his perseverance and dedication to this project. If everyone gave back to their communities just a fraction of what Bert does each year, the world would be a far better place. Peter would also like to thank Steve Roling for introducing him to Bert many years ago.

About the Authors

Bert Berkley (Kansas City, MO) is chairman of Tension Envelope Corporation, one of the nation's largest envelope manufacturers, and is the founder and immediate past chairman of the Local Investment Commission (LINC). He has made numerous presentations on the LINC model across the country and around the world, including the Netherlands, Israel, and Taiwan. Berkley served on the board of the Kauffman Center for Entrepreneurial Leadership and is currently on the boards of the Institute for Educational Leadership and Centerpoint for Leaders (both in Washington, D.C.) as well as state of Missouri and several local boards.

Peter Economy (La Jolla, CA) is a professional business writer and author or coauthor of the bestselling *Managing For Dummies* (Wiley—17 languages, more than 400,000 copies sold worldwide), *Enterprising Non-profits: A Toolkit for Social Entrepreneurs* (Wiley), *The Management Bible* (Wiley), *The SAIC Solution: How We Built an $8 Billion Employee-Owned Technology Company* (Wiley), and many others. He is also associate editor of *Leader to Leader,* the Apex award–winning publication of the Leader to Leader Institute. Visit his Web site at www.petereconomy.com.

Introduction

Stores across the country—including Build-a-Bear Workshop, the Discovery Channel, and Nike—are selling those ubiquitous yellow Lance Armstrong Live Strong wristbands (more than 70 million sold to date) for $1, the proceeds of which go toward cancer research. New York City's ABC Carpet & Home sold water buffaloes a few holiday seasons ago for $135 each, including delivery to a village in Cambodia. At the Gap, you could buy a teddy bear for $20, with a significant portion of the sales price dedicated to the company's goal of distributing 70,000 coats to disadvantaged North American children.

These are but a few examples of a groundswell in businesses that are giving back cited in a *New York Times* article titled "Stores Are Hoping to Do Well by Urging Shoppers to Do Good." And it's true—there is something new happening out there; more businesses than ever before are participating in charitable activities. As Craig R. Johnston, a retail consultant at Customer Growth Partners says, "Such retail-hosted charitable events and promotions have at least tripled since 2000, and have clearly accelerated in the past year."

The examples are all around us: boxes of General Mills Lucky Charms cereal emblazoned with American Heart Association "heart-check marks"; Wal-Mart's partnership with the Veterans of Foreign Wars Foundation to provide 900,000 communications kits to servicemen and -women (including free phone cards, writing paper, and envelopes) to help them stay in touch with loved ones; and BMW's $1 donations to the Susan G. Komen Breast Cancer Foundation for every test drive of the automobile manufacturer's products.

What exactly is going on here?

Are charitable activities such as these simply a thinly veiled ploy to pump sales by leveraging customer emotions? Is this just a momentary blip on the radar screen of today's business leaders, soon to be replaced by business as usual? Or are companies—and the men and women who work there, and those who run them—moving toward a new age of enlightenment, one where *giving back* is not just positive public relations, but essential to the way that they do business (and, indeed, to their future success)?

In his book *Bowling Alone* (Simon & Schuster, 1980), Robert Putnam indicates that the generation now in its 20s is the first generation since the one that is now it its 60s and over who are increasingly interested in volunteerism and helping their fellow man. Business marketers—spotting this interest among the young—are looking for ways to use it. This has in turn sparked many of the business/charity programs that are showing up around the country, also encouraging business leaders to personally do more charity work—and become more visible doing it.

But for businesspeople who decide to give back, there is more to this trend than simply obtaining an edge in product marketing. According to Kent C. (Oz) Nelson, former chairman and CEO of United Parcel Service (UPS), and past chairman of the Annie E. Casey Foundation, companies that do good in their communities also reap the following benefits:

- Companies that do good experience increased employee pride and morale, resulting in better performance and customer service (and an enhanced bottom line).
- Charitable activities can enhance a company's brand.
- Companies with good reputations are highly regarded by investors, including their own shareholders.
- Customers prefer to do business with companies that are known for the good work they do.

As it turns out, while the trend toward doing good has recently seen a sharp increase, businesspeople have done much over the years to contribute to society beyond running their companies. For example, a study of the United Way organization throughout the country would identify thousands of business leaders who have made significant contributions to their communities. There are countless other examples in a variety of other organizations, such as the American Cancer Society, Red

Cross, Boys and Girls Clubs of America, Big Brothers–Big Sisters, and on and on.

They do this for a reason. While some may have found these volunteer opportunities on their own, many others joined in after being "recruited" by leaders in nonprofits reaching out to the business community. Giving back, after all, is a partnership—a two-way street—and both sides of the equation play vital roles in the process.

We are fortunate to have the cooperation of a number of business leaders who have agreed to tell their stories for inclusion in this book. These leaders—whose stories, anecdotes, and personal observations, experience, and advice are woven into the chapters that follow—include:

- Roger Brown and Linda Mason, cofounders of Horizons for Homeless Children
- S. Truett Cathy, founder and chairman, Chick-fil-A, Inc.
- Matt Flannery, co-founder, Kiva.org
- Gary Hirshberg, chairman, president, and CEO of Stonyfield Farm
- Kent C. (Oz) Nelson, former chairman and CEO of United Parcel Service

Our hope is that this book will become a catalyst of change for businesspeople who want to have a positive and long-lasting impact in their communities, and on the world around them. It is our intention that, after reading this book, you'll be inspired to join us—and to write your own stories of giving back to your community. From our many years of experience in business—and in giving back—there will never be a shortage of problems to be solved, and there will always be a need for talented and passionate people to help solve them. Please let us know how it goes.

CHAPTER 1

Giving Back: Good For You, Your Business, and Your Community

No one has ever become poor by giving.

—ANNE FRANK

On August 29, 2005, the largest natural disaster in recorded American history wreaked havoc on Louisiana, Mississippi, and Alabama—three of the country's poorest states. The devastation was widespread—covering an area roughly the size of the entire United Kingdom, including the New Orleans metropolitan area, home to some 1.3 million people—and the number of people whose lives were impacted was enormous. All told, government estimates peg the number of people who suffered some form of personal loss—loss of property, loss of job, loss of shelter, loss of health, and loss of life—at more than 2 million people.

And though the jury is still out regarding the speed and the intensity of the government's response in the immediate aftermath of the storm, there are many inspiring stories of people and organizations jumping in with both feet to do whatever they could do to help those who most needed it. And many of these stories are of businesses—and the business-people who work there, and those who own and run them. Within a week after the disaster, Ameriquest pledged $5 million toward hurricane relief efforts, ExxonMobil $2 million, General Electric $6 million, Freddie Mac $10.1 million, and Toyota $5 million. And this is just a small sliver of the list of organizations and people that freely gave their time, their labor, their facilities, and most needed of all—their money—to make a difference in the world around them.

In short, to give back.

Today, in the United States of America, there's a change in the air—a change that promises to have significant and long-lasting impacts on our nation, our institutions, and our people. More than ever before, businesses—and the businesspeople who work there and who own and run them—are seeking new ways to get involved in their communities by affiliating with charities and nonprofits in meaningful and deeply powerful new ways. Here are just a few examples:

- Reflecting a fundamental change in attitude for Silicon Valley venture capital companies, investments in fledging companies that "make money by doing good" are up sharply. Even the billboards along Highway 101—which slices through the area—have changed. Instead of ads for pre-dot-com meltdown firms like Excite.com, Homestead .com, or eGain.com, billboards now urge its readers to "End World Hunger" and to support the men and women of the California National Guard, who "keep America safe, secure, and free."

- Through www.benevolink.com, a percentage of the sales of more than 150 online retailers is directed to any one of more than 1 million different charitable and nonprofit organizations. Online retailers (and their percentages of sales contributed) include: Nike (6.5%), Home Depot (2.5%), Gap (3%), Neiman Marcus (3%), FTD.com (20%), and Sony (3%).

- When it comes to serving the communities in which it operates, Wal-Mart Stores, Inc. puts its money where its mouth is, contributing more than $270 million to support its 4,000-plus U.S.-based communities in 2006. According to the *Chronicle of Philanthropy,* Wal-Mart is the largest corporate cash contributor in the United States.

So, why do businesses—and businesspeople—choose to give back to their communities? First, giving back is smart business—there are plenty of positive, immediate, and downstream impacts to make engaging in community service and community building the right thing to do for the businesses that do it. For example, if these activities produce safer communities (for workers and their families by reducing crime or improving working conditions), a better-educated workforce, improved educational scores and better school results, and healthier citizens, then the cascading financial effects for area businesses will be positive. Businesses will have safer communities in which to operate and locate, and they will be able to attract and retain higher-quality workers who will want to put down deep roots—resulting in more stable communities and less worker turnover.

Second, for many businesspeople, giving back is something that is important to them personally. A group of 10,983 Harvard Business School (HBS) alumni (a group with a demographic skewed toward extremely busy people with highly demanding jobs) was asked to rate the importance of their involvement with nonprofit organizations, with zero being "unimportant" and four being "very important." The average score for these alumni was 3.5, almost the maximum. A large percentage (81%) of these HBS alumni report being involved with nonprofits, while almost half of these business-people—42%—dedicate more than 10 hours a month to their nonprofit activities. When asking why businesspeople seem to naturally be drawn to community service, the most common answer is because they want to "make a difference." The words of one of the survey respondents—a bank senior vice president—are typical: "I hope that I can turn and say I didn't just serve, but I made some meaningful contributions."[1]

A LONG TRADITION OF GIVING BACK

Americans have a long tradition of giving back in their communities, but the number of citizens actually participating in them—and the extent of their participation—has been on a steady decline since the early 1900s, when the great institutions of federal government (and the resultant professional corps of bureaucrats and functionaries) were designed and institutionalized. The growth of this bureaucracy—and the resultant growth of massive government social programs—led citizens to become increasingly reliant on *government* to solve their problems, and less reliant on *themselves*.

It wasn't always this way. In his book *Democracy in America,* Frenchman Alexis de Tocqueville related the following observations of American life in the 1830s:

> Americans of all ages, all stations of life, and all types of dispositions are forever forming associations. There are not only commercial and industrial associations in which all take part, but others of a thousand different

types—religious, moral, serious, futile, very general and very limited, immensely large and very minute. . . . Nothing strikes a European traveler in the United States more than the absence of what we would call government or administration. There is nothing centralized or hierarchic in the constitution of American administrative power.

This is not to say that the government played no role in the United States at that time—it did play an important role in national defense, international commerce, and the building of infrastructure such as roads and a postal system—but what most impressed de Tocqueville was the American penchant for citizen initiative and involvement, forming groups to solve problems in their communities and to help each other without any direction from government. When it came to the issues that had the greatest impact on the daily life of individual citizens, citizen interest and engagement in the development of solutions was quite high.

We don't think anyone today would accuse the United States of having an absence of government or centralized administration. Since those early days of our nation, the term *big* government has become synonymous with our federal government—and for very good reason. The annual budget of the U.S. government is more than $2.3 trillion, which goes to support a wide array of organizations, programs, and services that touch the lives of each and every American citizen. And, while the federal government directly employs only about 1.7 million civilians (plus a couple million more in the uniformed military and postal service), this number rises dramatically—to about 17 million people—when one considers the nonfederal employees who work under federal contracts and grants.

According to the Brookings Institution's Paul Light, this "shadow of government"—which is charged with all sorts of tasks, from peeling potatoes for the Department of Defense, to running Indian schools for the Bureau of Indian Affairs, to opening tax returns for the Internal Revenue Service—has grown dramatically over the past 30 years, and it plays an increasingly important role in the lives of each and every American citizen. And this is just the federal government; there are many millions more people employed by state and local governments all across the nation.

This huge bureaucracy—aided and abetted by state and local governments, and countless government-sponsored agencies, commissions, and task forces—has played a key role in dramatically decreasing citizen self-reliance and in disengaging people from decision making in their communities. Fortunately, this disengagement is being increasingly fought by a new vanguard of businesses and the businesspeople who work there, and those who own and run them.

THE ADVANTAGES OF ENGAGED CITIZENS

The simple fact is this: Members of a community—families, providers, agencies, businesses, community groups, and other local partners—are in a much better position to understand exactly what it is they need than are people who do not live in that community, no matter how well intentioned they may be. Not only that, but because members of a community are directly impacted by the effects of the decisions that they make—often for an entire lifetime, they have a vested interest in making sure that they are implemented effectively.

There are two key advantages of an engaged citizenry:

First, by increasing the diversity of input into the decision-making process, the decisions that result are actually better ones. Why? Because no one person—and no single group or constituency or business or government agency or department—has a monopoly on the best solution to every possible issue or problem. And no one person or entity has a monopoly on new and creative ways to leverage or take advantage of opportunities as they arise. Everyone in a community has *something* to contribute to the process, and everyone in a community should be invited and encouraged to do just that.

Second, engaging citizens in the decision-making process enhances social capital by broadening constituencies and stakeholders. Social capital is a set of resources (norms, networks, traditions) that helps to solve problems by collective action, and that builds goodwill and trust. When people in a community have a voice in decisions that affect them, they suddenly see themselves (and, others see them) as a vital part of the solution. Indeed, they are. Self-respect and self-confidence are raised, as are communication, goodwill, and trust among the different constituencies and stakeholders.

And while the focus of the move to local governance has traditionally been on the partnership between government and community, this thinking has been changing in recent years. The local governance (community decision making) has become an opportunity for citizens to build the types of networks of support (both formal and informal) that may actually prevent children and families from needing to seek out public agency help. The need for public services—however good they may be—indicates in most cases that something went wrong somewhere for an individual or family.

By establishing a group of citizens who are willing to take on the responsibility to monitor community-wide conditions and results and then to convene, motivate, and cajole others to care "with them" about addressing those results, community decision making can become a proactive strategy for insuring good individual and community health. In these instances, the group may not have been started by a public agency, and it may focus on results that are not necessarily aligned with a public agency agenda. Further, the group would not be intimidated by a government agency.

The goal becomes one of an improved quality of life for a community so that the community might increase its chances of contributing to the healthy development of children and families who live within it. Furthermore, citizens give this work legitimacy because—unlike public agencies—they are motivated by the fact that they are attempting to improve their own lives and the overall community's health.

How Businesspeople Give Back

There are a number of different ways that businesspeople give back to their communities. And, although some require that the businessperson who is giving back apply a significant amount of personal wealth to get the initiative off the ground, that is not always the case. In fact, some approaches require nothing more than a person's time, talent, and energy.

Here are some of the most common ways businesspeople give back:

- Donate money (such as when Warren Buffett decided in 2006 to donate more than $30 billion of his stock to the Bill & Melinda Gates Foundation).
- Direct company resources (such as the $270 million+ that Wal-Mart executives directed the company to contribute to philanthropic causes in the United States in 2006).

- Start a foundation (such as Chicago's Comer Foundation—started by Lands' End founder Gary Comer—which provides funding to Chicago-area nonprofits in the fields of culture, education, environment, health, and social services).
- Start a nonprofit organization (such as the nonprofit A-T Children's Project in Deerfield Beach, Florida—founded by biotech executive Brad Margus—which is dedicated to finding a cure for the rare degenerative disease ataxia-telangiectasia).
- Start a company with a community mission (such as Benevolink—founded by Tunstall Rushton—which helps consumers give to their favorite charities through the act of shopping).
- Start a quasi-governmental agency (such as LINC—the Local Investment Commission in Kansas City, Missouri, founded by businessman and coauthor of this book, Bert Berkley—which acts as an intermediary between the state of Missouri and the citizens of Kansas City).
- Donate time and expertise (such as the group of 50 Rhode Island real estate agents who volunteered to build homes for Habitat for Humanity to be delivered to victims of Hurricane Katrina on the Gulf Coast).
- Act as a catalyst for change (such as Peter Economy's community action that—together with the collective action of hundreds of others who decided to break away from the Special Olympics organization—led to the founding of San Diego's SPORTS for Exceptional Athletes).
- Be a volunteer (such as the thousands of Home Depot employees who each year volunteer to build playgrounds for children, repair homes for the elderly, help inner-city teens learn job skills, educate customers about energy usage, and much more through the company's Team Depot Project 1-2-3 program).

While these are not the only ways businesspeople can give back to their communities, they are perhaps among the most common. If you are thinking of giving back, then, chances are your approach will match one of these categories. Remember: You can have a measurable and lasting impact on your community, even if you don't have a lot of money (or even *any* money) to devote to your cause. Just your time, your skills, and your passion can make all the difference in the world.

Looking Forward

As we have seen in this chapter, businesses and businesspeople can and are making a major difference in their communities—becoming considerably more engaged in them and bringing about the kind of change that used to be the sole province of big government. Increasingly, giving back is being seen not just as good business (imbuing businesses with a (public relations) PR-friendly halo of righteousness), but as *smart* business—creating economic value for these organizations and their shareholders.

In the chapters that follow, we will take a close look at a number of businesspeople who have given back to their communities—often in very dramatic ways. Some of these businesspeople were top executives when they started their giving habit, and some weren't. Some had a lot of money to devote to their causes, and others did not. In every case, we will show you how motivated and visionary businesspeople are bringing about fundamental and lasting changes in their communities—making peoples' lives better—and the very good business reasons for doing so.

We challenge you to join these men and women, because just as they have given back, so can you.

Note

1. James E. Austin, "Business Leaders and Nonprofits." Working paper, Harvard Business School, 1997.

CHAPTER 2

The LINC Between Business and Community in Kansas City

In Kansas City, Missouri, there is occurring a quiet but startling revolution in the administration of human services funded by the state and federal government. It ranks as a major breakthrough in American governance.

—JOHN GARDNER, FOUNDER, COMMON CAUSE

The state of Missouri is truly blessed. The "Show Me" state—Gateway to the West, and home to two of the greatest rivers in North America, the Mississippi and Missouri—boasts stunning scenery, big-city excitement, and small-town charm, as well as music, arts, history, and heritage. Its two largest cities—St. Louis and Kansas City—are among the nation's most cosmopolitan, and the state is home to such business giants as Anheuser-Busch, Hallmark Cards, Emerson, Graybar Electric, and others.

But underneath all this natural beauty and seeming prosperity, there is a different tale to tell—one of missed opportunities, financial hardship, and people doing whatever it takes to put food on the table and keep a roof over their heads and provide for their health care needs. Missouri suffers from widespread poverty—both in its poor, rural areas and in its decaying urban centers—and violent crime has been a long-term problem for the state.

Statistics from the late 1980s and early 1990s show how serious the problems of poverty, lack of education, and crime were in Missouri.

It was evident that a catalyst for change was needed. Fortunately, such an organization came on the scene. The name of the organization was (and is today) the Local Investment Commission (LINC), which has nothing to do with stocks and bonds, but everything to do with investing in children and families, and letting those in local communities have an active role in the decisions that affect them.

The founder of LINC is Bert Berkley, chairman of the board of Tension Envelope Corporation, a family business started in 1886 by his grandfather. The story of his grandfather is worth telling, as he was a true entrepreneur. He was a small businessman in Pittsburgh, Pennsylvania, selling advertising novelties. When he made a little money, he would invest in real estate. One day he made a mistake. He signed a note for a friend who subsequently went broke.

Bert's grandfather sold his real estate, paid off the note, decided to leave Pittsburgh, and found his way to Kansas City, where he started selling advertising novelties. On his sales calls he learned that envelopes came from manufacturers in Chicago and St. Louis. He went east and brought the first envelope folding machines west of St. Louis, Missouri.

His two sons successfully carried on the business. Today, Tension has eight manufacturing plants in the United States, as well as factories in Taiwan, China, Malaysia, and Australia. Bert's son is president and chief executive officer, representing the fourth generation of the family to head the business.

The ironic part of the story is that the Pittsburgh property Bert's grandfather sold to pay off his friend's debt is now the Golden Triangle of downtown Pittsburgh.

Bert attended Duke University for two years, at which time he was called into service for World War II. He served for 42 months, including 11 months in the Philippines. Upon graduation from Duke, he went to Harvard Business School, and because of his reserve status at the time of graduation he was called back into the Army and went to Korea, where he was a first lieutenant in the infantry. He received the Combat Infantry Badge and was awarded the Bronze Star. Bert promised himself that if he got out of Korea alive, he would give back.

Upon returning from Korea, having served in both wars a total of 59 months, he went to work for Tension Envelope Corporation. He has been a community volunteer ever since.

THE STATISTICAL PROOF/STATE OF AFFAIRS THEN

In 1989, approximately 350,000 households—almost 18% of the total households in the state of Missouri (1.9 million)—had an annual income of less than $10,000.[1] In Jackson County—the county in which Kansas City is located—more than 41,000 households, or 16.5%, had annual incomes of less than $10,000.[2] To get some idea of exactly what that means, in 1989, a family of four was considered to be in poverty if annual income dipped below $12,674.[3]

But, while there's no doubt that the nationwide recession of the late 1980s and early 1990s had something to do with this lack of financial opportunity and for the endemic poverty in which one in five Missouri households found themselves, a lack of academic achievement surely had a significant impact as well. Out of 3.2 million Missourians 25 years of age and over in 1989, 380,000 men and women—12% of the total— had attained less than a ninth-grade education, while another 478,000 (14.5%) made it to high school, but never received a diploma.[4] While better than the average for the rest of the state, almost 7% of Kansas City residents 25 years of age and over had less than a 9th grade education, and another 14% attended high school, but did not receive a diploma.[5] In an economy increasingly hungry for workers with at least some proficiency in the new information technologies, this left many Missourians—and Kansas Citians—firmly planted on the list of have-nots.

And, this lack of opportunity led to another unfortunate outcome— crime. A decade ago, Kansas City, Missouri, was ranked only 32nd in population among U.S. cities; it had the 8th highest crime rate in the nation. And St. Louis—the 38th most populous city in the United States—had the 5th highest crime rate in the nation.[6]

Added to this mix were the aftereffects of decades of racial discrimination and segregation. On April 9, 1968, a few days after the assassination of Martin Luther King Jr., violence erupted in Kansas City when the school district refused to close city schools for a day. In addition to the city's 900-man police force, 1,700 National Guardsmen, and 168 Missouri state troopers were finally able to quell the riot six days later; two people were killed, 44 were injured, and 175 were arrested. And, although the federal government mandated the desegregation of public schools starting in the 1950s, Kansas City didn't put a plan into effect until 1984. When that plan failed, a court-ordered plan was mandated in 1990.

It was not that the federal government and the state of Missouri weren't trying to help—they were. By fiscal year 1993, the federal government was sending more than $477 million a year to Missouri for food stamps, $515 million in unemployment compensation benefit payments, $362 million for lower-income housing assistance, $3.5 billion for Medicare, and hundreds of millions more for a variety of other social programs.[7] The state of Missouri did its part as well, funneling $294 million into an assortment of social programs in fiscal year 1994, including child care assistance, job training programs, early childhood education, and other initiatives to help poor families beat the cycle of poverty.[8]

The problem was this: These programs—administered from more than 100 miles away (Missouri's capital is in Jefferson City), or from more than 1,000 miles away (in the case of the nation's capital of Washington, D.C.)—just were not getting the job done. The thought was there—as were the dollars—but the hoped-for results were notably absent.

THE DEPARTMENT OF SOCIAL SERVICES

In Missouri, the Department of Social Services (DSS) was responsible for distributing state and federal funding to organizations that run the social programs meant to enable poor and disadvantaged citizens to rise out of poverty—and their children, and their children's children.

The DSS mission statement describes the organization's reason to exist:

> To maintain or improve the quality of life for the people of the state of Missouri by providing the best possible services to the public, with respect, responsiveness, and accountability, which will enable individuals and families to better fulfill their potential.

The DSS—created in 1974 to serve as an umbrella agency—fulfills its mission by coordinating programs to provide public assistance to children and their parents, access to health care, services to the elderly, child support enforcement assistance, and specialized assistance to troubled youth. With some 8,500 employees, working with an annual budget of approximately $5 billion, DSS provides financial assistance and services to those

Missourians most in need, while working to strengthen families and move them from dependency to self-sufficiency.

Unfortunately, in the late 1980s, like many other large government bureaucracies, the DSS was out of touch with the citizens it was supposed to serve, and its programs didn't meet their most critical needs.

According to one observer at the time:

> The Department of Social Services didn't do many things. They studied a lot, they worked at a lot of things, but they did not take action. Certainly, if the press roasted someone in the department for some shortcoming, they would take action. But as far as making definitive changes to the system—and that's the key, making changes to the system—it just didn't happen.

Because of their nature, most bureaucracies—and the people within them—see the impersonal application of rules, regulations, and procedures as their highest priority, not the delivery of the services for which they were created in the first place. Eventually, organizations like this begin to serve themselves rather than the communities in which they do business. When bureaucracies become dysfunctional, they exhibit a number of symptoms, including:

- Officials become out of touch and arrogant.
- Individuals focus on protecting themselves and on increasing the power of their positions.
- Administrative systems (policies, procedures, and so forth) become ends unto themselves.
- Program outcomes receive little administrative attention.
- Major policy change or adjustment, or true genuine system reform, is difficult, absent some major political upheaval or scandal.

Without a doubt, the Missouri DSS was dysfunctional. The patient was not yet terminal, but it was showing all the signs of debilitating chronic illness. According to Herman Johnson, a two-term state representative in the Missouri General Assembly, LINC commissioner, and vice chair since LINC's founding in 1992:

> It had gotten to the point that the Division of Family Services [a division of DSS] was for the professionals who worked there, and not for the people that they were supposed to serve. In one case that really

bothered me, a lady had been down to the Division of Family Service, a division of DSS, to apply for some benefit that they had. They told her that she wasn't eligible, so she went away. Then someone else told her, "Well, no, you're not eligible for that, but you are eligible for this." So, when she goes back to the social worker who was processing her application, and the supervisor confirmed that the client was eligible for the other program, the social worker said, "Well, she didn't ask for that."

Before LINC came to be, there were a number of attempts to change the way that DSS did business. Each attempt, however, met strenuous resistance by those within the bureaucracy who were threatened by prospect of change—and there were many in the organization who found themselves in that particular camp. According to Steve Winburn, a former, long-time employee of the DSS Division of Youth Services, and current member of LINC's Health and Child Welfare Committee staff:

Prior to LINC, there were two different attempts from the state to combine certain services internally, and there would be a big push and a whole lot of energy around making that happen. But state employees would soon get scared by that—because it was something new and unknown—and, even though there was all this activity, and all these things going on, nothing would happen. Invariably, something would fall through and that would be that.

The winds of change were blowing, however, and things soon would not be the same for DSS. Concerned about stories of welfare fraud and rampant abuse of government entitlements, the American public began to demand change—both to the social programs that constituted so much of the nation's annual budget, and to the bureaucracies that were charged with administering these programs.

The *smart* leaders—including Gary Stangler, DSS's then director—saw this change coming, and knew their organizations would have to adapt, finding better ways to do their jobs and to meet the needs of their communities in the process. But the path wasn't an obvious one; it took a lot of work, perseverance, and willingness to take risks on the part of a lot of people to bring about these changes.

The lines of change, both within the Department of Social Services, and in the community, were beginning to converge. While neither side yet knew they were about to join forces, it was increasingly clear that the time was ripe for change. All that was needed was some forum that would bring the two sides together. This was soon found in an unlikely place: the DSS Business Roundtable.

BERT BERKLEY AND THE BUSINESS ROUNDTABLE

One of the problems with bureaucracies like the Missouri DSS is that they tend to become isolated from the constituents they are supposed to serve. Instead of reaching out to their communities in search of feedback on their service delivery, or to solicit new ideas that will improve the way they do business, government agencies tend to become very reactive—focusing their efforts on maintaining the status quo and avoiding the kind of controversy that tends to land them on the front page of the newspapers or the hard-hitting investigative report on local television.

Gary Stangler realized, however, that if he was going to bring about his dream of making a bold change in DSS, he would have to solicit the support of others outside the agency—isolation was *not* the pathway to success. To achieve this goal, Stangler devised an innovative way to bring key members of the business community together with those in DSS who hoped to push the agenda of change through the system. The result was the DSS Business Roundtable. Stangler recalls:

> I came up with this notion of a business roundtable. I met early on with Charlie Hucker at Hallmark, and I found that businesspeople, in general, are very interested in their community and they need only be asked. Once asked, they feel somewhat empowered and more important. This is where I began to understand the importance of nurturing these relationships in the business community because they were nontraditional to the social services. The name Bert Berkley came up several times, so I decided I needed to meet him. I went to see Bert, and he very diligently took notes throughout my entire conversation— just before I had to give a speech that day at a United Way function. Later, somebody came up to me at the lunch and said, "Bert Berkley called about you. He wanted to know who you were and if you were for real." It turned out that he, in that very short time, had begun checking me out, deciding whether or not he should be a part of the Roundtable.

Because of the recession that gripped the nation and the state of Missouri in the late 1980s and early 1990s, and because of the resultant cutbacks in government funding, Gary Stangler was worried about how his agency was going to maintain health care for the poor. What was needed was a strong core of advocates who could help him push his agenda through the system. And, because he understood that advocates are made and not born, he scheduled the first meeting of the Business Roundtable at Children's Hospital in Saint Louis. This meeting pretty much sealed the deal for all who attended. Says Stangler:

> I led everyone to the neonatal ward, and this was when Bert held a preemie in his hand. From that moment, Bert was fully committed to the agenda.

The Business Roundtable brought together nine people from across the state, all with one goal in mind: to take a close look at the DSS and see how it could be run better. Over a period of many months, participants received a liberal education on everything the Department did—how it accounted for welfare mothers, how it administered food stamp programs, how it worked with local medical facilities, and much, much more.

Indeed, the decision to invite Bert Berkley to join the Business Round-table was a fortuitous one. The more Bert learned about how the system worked (or, in many cases, actually, how it failed to work), the more frustrated he became. Critical social service decisions for Kansas City were being made in Jefferson City by people who had precious little knowledge of the impact of those decisions on the community. As time went on—and as the status quo remained just that—Bert began to voice his frustrations to a growing number of friends and colleagues. But, even more important, Bert Berkley began to search for solutions to the Department's problems—solutions that would provide better services to those in Kansas City who needed them most by fundamentally changing the way DSS did business.

SuEllen Fried, an author and speaker on the topic of child abuse and bullying, a LINC commissioner, and co-chair of the LINC Quality Serv-ices Committee, each time she saw Bert, asked how things were going with the Roundtable. After explaining what was going on, Bert asked about her activities. She reported that the Coalition for the Prevention of Child Abuse in the state of Kansas was considering allowing people from a small community to decide how to best use the money to prevent child abuse. At that moment, Bert said, "SuEllen, you may have just opened the doors."

After that meeting with SuEllen Fried, Bert Berkley devoted the better part of the next couple of weeks to developing a plan for a new kind of organization, the Local Investment Commission—LINC. Soon, Berkley called Gary Stangler and asked if he would drop by his office the next time he was in Kansas City. When Stangler arrived a couple of days later, Berkley laid out the entire structure for LINC, what the organization would do, how it would operate, the committees that would be formed—*everything*.

Stangler's response? "Good idea, let's try it." To Gary Stangler's credit, at that time, he may have been the only person in his position in the country with the vision to understand that extending control of several hundred million dollars and entrusting them to the citizens of Kansas City would result in better, more effective decisions. He realized that controlling less and allowing citizens to decide more was the way of the future.

The Commission of ordinary citizens was made up of a broad cross-section of Kansas Citians, including business leaders, labor leaders, community volunteers, African-Americans, Hispanics, Caucasians, men, women, the elderly, and youth.

Bert understood that ordinary citizens had only limited understanding of how the distribution of social services worked, and the commissioners and committee members would need competent professional advice. Professional cabinets were established for the Commission, and for each committee. A cabinet member is a government or not-for-profit professional who has broad community experience (for the Commission), or for each committee—professionals who have knowledge of the committee's responsibilities, such as health care.

The cabinet members are asked to be at each meeting, not just when invited. They do not have a vote, but they each have a voice, and the voice is extremely important.

The vision of what would soon become LINC was based on three key beliefs: (1) that things could be changed—people did not have to accept the status quo and, just because something had "always" been done a particular way didn't mean that it couldn't be changed; (2) that broad citizen involvement, including citizen decision making, would create an impetus for change; and (3) that what needed to be done was readily apparent and required only a small amount of additional study and planning before taking action.

The slogan of choice was, and is, "READY—FIRE—AIM," meaning take an intense but short-term look at the problem, determine what should be done to improve or change the situation ("READY"), and then do it, take action ("FIRE"). Observe progress, and continually make changes to improve the original action plan ("AIM"). READY—FIRE—AIM.

MAKING THE LEAP—LINC

Amazingly enough—especially considering all the reasons why it would have been safer for the careers of DSS officials and staff to maintain the status quo, regardless of whether or not it was working—the idea of LINC began to gain traction. And, as it did, a number of people began to imagine that this crazy idea just might make a lot of sense—and that it might actually come to pass.

As DSS began the process of change, Bert Berkley continued to refine his idea of LINC and local control over federal and state social services funding. He talked to many people about his plan, winning a growing group of allies that would be important in the struggles that lay ahead. According to Bob Rogers, former chairman of the Ewing Marion Kauffman Foundation, and a former LINC commissioner, Mr. Kauffman was very intrigued by the idea, seeing it as a way to make a real and lasting change in people's lives, and in the way that government worked with citizens. In the words of Bob Rogers:

> Bert and Mr. Kauffman had an early conversation about the idea of LINC and, to use a well-used expression, it blew Mr. Kauffman away. He said, "Wow! This is significant—this is a new way of really taking care of the issue as opposed to funding the same thing over and over again without any result." He wrote a blank check for Bert. He said, "What do you need?"

Besides paying for LINC's very first office space, the Kauffman Foundation's early and ongoing financial help in paying for training and other support became a critical element in the eventual success of the organization. Still, there was no guarantee that this new entity called LINC would be able to change the world, or even a small part of it. According to Steve Winburn:

> There were mixed feelings from the community about what LINC would be and how it would fit into the overall community system. Would it truly make a difference in people's lives, or would it turn out to be just another layer of bureaucracy? People were not satisfied with the way the state system worked—I don't think anybody truly was. Even the state workers weren't satisfied. Some were wary of change, but others said, "We've got a chance to change the delivery of social service—let's do it."

LINC was born when Gary Stangler issued a letter authorizing the Commission, with the sole limitation that the group could not do anything that was immoral or illegal. LINC's structure, authority, staff, and schedule were spelled out in a manner that empowered the Commission to find its own way.

LINC was set up as a state-chartered entity, an arm of the state of Missouri. When DSS made the decision to entrust LINC with indirect control of hundreds of millions of dollars that it sent each year to Kansas City, it set the stage for a multitude of programs to follow. The ability to access state funds for the Caring Communities Initiative, to have flexible funding to support community-based initiatives, to be a pioneer in welfare reform, its role in Title IV-E foster care and subsidized adoption reimbursement (which provided an important source of flexible resources for LINC to draw from), the Child Health Insurance Program (CHIP), and Educare (which provides training and resources primarily to home-based child care providers)—all became part of the unique and comprehensive partnership that the state of Missouri developed with LINC.

Jim Koeneman, then a senior program officer with the Ewing Marion Kauffman Foundation's Youth Development Board, and a member of the LINC professional cabinet, recalls the excitement and promise of this quiet revolution:

> The whole idea was to get local communities much more involved in the design and implementation of state and other funded social services programs. There was something like 325 or 350 million dollars of DSS money coming into the community every year, and now we're going to have the opportunity to do something with those dollars and give direction from the community.

In its original incarnation—before the appointment of commissioners and before official meetings commenced—the LINC organization was structured to have people in the neighborhoods come together to determine what services were needed, and what problems needed to be solved. They would then work with the Commission and LINC committee members to bring about change.

Although Bert understood that changing the methods of operation of an 8,500-person department would be difficult, he did not understand the enormity of the roadblocks that would be put in his way and in the way of Gayle Hobbs, the original executive director who has since been elevated to president of LINC.

Gary Stangler, director of the DSS, made an individual available to help write up the ways LINC in Kansas City would work with the various divisions of DSS. Bert was given one excuse after another as to why the work was not progressing. Finally, Bert called Gary Stangler and said, "You're going to have to choose between him and me." Gary chose Bert. Forward movement started and continued.

When it became evident that Gary and Bert were going to bring about changes, certain prominent members of the Kansas City community came to see Bert to attempt to convince him that allowing ordinary citizens to make decisions would be detrimental, particularly when the decision makers were not trained social workers. Bert listened attentively, then explained that those in Kansas City know more about what is needed, and would be here to follow up to see that various not-for-profit agencies which do and do not receive money from the state were being effective in bringing their services to the neighborhoods.

Each of these situations was discussed with Gary Stangler, who had issued a directive to cooperate with LINC. In a number of cases Gary had a talk with the uncooperative individual, and the situation was corrected.

There were naysayers, and Bert and Gayle had many individual discussions with DSS members in Jefferson City and those stationed in Kansas City. Also, together or separately they made presentation after presentation about LINC to Kansas City organizations spelling out the advantages of local involvement and local control. Reaction was favorable.

According to Gayle Hobbs, president of LINC: "Many talented and committed people were working for the DSS. They knew the difficulties that they faced daily. They also knew what many of the solutions might be. But, as with many large organizations, the financial, political, and human resources were not always aligned to realize those solutions. LINC gave them the vehicle to make changes, be valued, be heard, and improve results. Poor results were no longer just an agency problem but a community problem. It was quite a sight to see: The results were real and shared by everyone."

Through the enlightened work of Landon Rowland, former chairman of Kansas City Southern Railroad, and Gayle Hobbs, chairman of LINC, Candace Cheatam, deputy director of LINC, Brent Schondelmeyer, communication director of LINC, and a highly competent staff of forty-four, which supports the citizen leadership of LINC, the organization has been highly successful, and has been recognized nationally and internationally.

Success has come about primarily because LINC is citizen driven, not staff driven. Commissioners and committee members remain committed because each one firmly believes he/she is changing people's lives for the better, and they are.

LINC's mission statement is: To provide leadership and influence to engage the Kansas City community in creating the best service delivery system to support and strengthen children, families, and individuals; holding that system accountable; and changing public attitudes towards the system.

It represents the firm foundation on which LINC was built and reflects the core of beliefs that drive the organization even today.

LINC carries out four critical functions: (1) engaging, convening, and supporting diverse groups and communities; (2) establishing quality standards and promoting accountability; (3) brokering and leveraging resources; and (4) promoting effective policy measures.

These efforts occur at two levels: LINC provides funding, support staff, data systems, and training for over 70 low-income neighborhood schools through partnerships with five school districts. At these schools, LINC organizes parents, neighbors, and businesses into site councils that are charged to direct neighborhood-level efforts. At the larger community level, LINC supports volunteer engagement with major policy issues—welfare-to-work, child welfare, health—bringing community knowledge to bear on state system reform efforts. This two-level approach involves over 2,100 volunteers—welfare mothers, neighborhood businesses, seniors, parents, corporation executives, faith-based organizations—in deciding how funds are spent in their neighborhoods, while creating an informed constituency to champion reform in statewide human service systems.

LINC is a striking example of how a citizen-led community intermediary can successfully coordinate the delivery of child, family, and senior supportive services while forging connections between neighborhoods and government agencies.

For a medium-size city, like Kansas City, to have over 2,100 volunteers on a year-round basis is noteworthy. Volunteers are the backbone of the organization. They determine what problems will be addressed, how solutions should be arrived at, and what actions should be taken, and then they take the responsibility to implement the solution. Staff is on hand to work closely with the volunteers. And that's the secret of LINC's success. Volunteers are making decisions, working with people in the neighborhoods, and creating meaningful, positive change.

Volunteers can also be helpful in working with legislators, particularly at the state level, to see that the constructive views of DSS are understood, and in some cases, acted upon.

Landon Rowland, LINC's chairman, stated:

> LINC is a "bottom-up" organization: We take our orders from people in the neighborhood, and the principal vehicle for our work in the community is through partnerships with neighborhood schools—an initiative called "Caring Communities." Bringing the community into the school is our goal. We identify resources of the community—resources that are always there but often overlooked—and bring them together in the schools, where parents, children, and neighbors can find their way to access needed services. Facilitating this neighborhood governance at each Caring Communities site is a manager called a site coordinator. Site coordinators are capable people, from all ethnic backgrounds, of every age. Through their activities, LINC works with a volunteer base of more than 2,100 parents and neighbors in six school districts and several charter schools.

But was the birth of LINC simply a fluke—a fortuitous set of circumstances that could not be easily replicated elsewhere—or was this a model for a new way of governing that could be applied to other communities? It is a model that can be replicated in other states and cities, as evidenced by the fact that in 20 counties in Missouri there are public-private partnerships modeled on LINC. Without a doubt, it requires an organized and concerted effort to get an initiative like LINC off the ground, and to make it fly. In the case of LINC, it took three key constituencies, all working together: government, business, and community.

Dr. Oscar Pinsker, former co-chair of the LINC Health Care Committee is a LINC commissioner, a practicing physician, and he has held leadership positions in a number of professional organizations. According to Pinsker:

> It's like creating a recipe for baking a cake—unless you have the basic ingredients, it's not going to work. In the case of LINC, the basic ingredients were two governors and the head of the Department of Social Services—Governor Ashcroft and Gary Stangler, as well as Governor Mel Carnahan, who wanted LINC to succeed. If you don't have that kind of push from the top, you're not going to make anything happen within the lower levels of the bureaucracy. And it took the influence and desire of business leaders—men like Bert Berkley and Landon Rowland. And, finally, and certainly not least, it took the leaders of the community that we were trying to serve—people like Rosemary Smith-Lowe and Herman Johnson.

While the spark that started LINC was by now quickly becoming a flame, it was still a very fragile thing. Any number of events—from a change in the management of DSS, to a change in the state's political climate, to a change in federal guidelines for the disbursement of funds—could have easily derailed LINC and sent it to the dustbin of good intentions that never made it to the Big League. But, the spark was lit, and all involved were committed to carrying this revolutionary idea to its logical next step. The excitement was palpable, and the tides of change were just beginning to rise.

In the 15 years since its founding, LINC's efforts have received widespread attention, having been cited on numerous occasions by then-President Bill Clinton as a model for other cities and states to emulate, and in the *New York Times,* the *Wall Street Journal,* the *Chronicle of Philanthropy,* and *USA Today* as the way that government should do business in the future. Here are just a few of the outstanding results that LINC has helped to bring about:

- Dramatically reduced welfare rolls in Jackson County. Even more important, the local recidivism rate—the number of people who return to welfare rolls—is only 16.7% in Jackson County, compared to 48% statewide and as high as 57% nationwide. LINC arranged for a DSS case worker to be assigned to each individual who went from welfare to work. If a problem developed on the job, the case-worker was called to help both parties—the company and the employee—find a practical solution.

- Improved academic results. Four schools in LINC's program had the highest Missouri Assessment Program reading scores in the entire school district.
- Rescued the troubled Extended Day program in the Kansas City, Missouri School District by securing new funding and providing better program support.
- Collected state and local data—broken down by zip code—enabling people to understand the real-world situation in their neighbor-hoods rather than rely on gut feelings.

The ongoing success of LINC proves that it is practical for ordinary citizens to come together to solve their own community problems.

CASESTUDY   A NEW APPROACH TO GOVERNANCE

In his report, "Working Better Together," R. Scott Fosler presents a new model of governance that reflects the new realities of social change. There are three new realities in Fosler's model:

1. *The public agenda is now jointly held.* Every sector of society recognizes that it has a role to play in making things better. Whether it is a corporation, nonprofit, church, or school, all need to be a part of the solution.
2. *Progress comes through consensus.* Cutting-edge communi-ties that have made progress have abandoned the old zero-sum model—I beat you today, you beat me tomorrow, I beat you the next day, you beat me the day after that—and have adopted a new process of focusing on shared values and ways of moving ahead together. They have discovered that progress comes through consensus.
3. *Many voices matter.* Everybody who is involved in an important decision, or is affected by it, needs to be at the table if you are to effect real change. Not only can this provide the basis for

consensus and a foundation for joint action, but if you don't include all the key constituencies, the excluded ones are likely to either stop the initiative or make life miserable for all those attempting to move it forward. It is especially important to include groups that have been excluded in the past, such as neighborhoods, women, people of color, and youth.[9]

LINC is a practical, living, vibrant example of how people can work together to create a civil society.

Q&A WITH BERT BERKLEY, FOUNDER OF THE LOCAL INVESTMENT COMMISSION (LINC) (KANSAS CITY, MISSOURI)

Giving Back: What event(s) took place that allowed you to decide you wanted to give back?

Bert Berkley: My mother and father were very active in the community, and both my paternal and maternal grandfathers were recognized in their city for outstanding contributions to the community. The idea of giving back was part of my upbringing. As a combat infantry first lieutenant in Korea, I promised that if I made it out alive I would give back. With so many whom I knew killed, I was the fortunate one who was not even wounded. Thus, I could fulfill my promise.

Giving Back: How old were you at the time?

Bert Berkley: I was 27 years old.

Giving Back: Did you have friends or acquaintances who discouraged you?

Bert Berkley: At the time I was doing research to determine whether or not I should attempt to start LINC, I talked with a number of people in government who told me it would not work, that the concept of structural change being made by civilians who knew nothing about the social services made the plan impractical, and I should stop wasting my time. After LINC was under way, some people attempted to persuade me not to go forward.

Giving Back: What is the most significant contribution you have made with your leadership skills?

Bert Berkley: Starting an organization from scratch, particularly one that involved both public and private entities, and embraced a concept that had never been started before, required someone who was dedicated to success, and was willing to involve others and spend the time needed to solve each new problem.

Giving Back: What is the most significant contribution you have made with your financial resources?

Bert Berkley: Money for LINC comes from the federal and state governments. Although I have contributed to the 501(c)3 created for LINC, my contributions have not been a major factor in LINC's financial success.

Giving Back: What was the objective of your project, and whom did you wish to benefit?

Bert Berkley: The objective of the project was to put local people in charge of determining where money for the social services would be spent, as those at the local level are much more familiar with where money is needed, and they are able to determine if it is being used to bring about desired results. It was my intent to benefit primarily, but not exclusively, those at lower economic levels who need help.

Giving Back: What changes, if any, would you make today in your initial approach?

Bert Berkley: For all practical purposes, I would make no changes, although there were individual instances with bureaucrats in Jefferson City, Missouri, that might have been handled a bit differently, but once their objections were overcome, we received the kind of cooperation we wanted. The same is true of local Kansas Citians who wanted to stop LINC in its infancy, but once they understood LINC's leadership was determined to make the concept successful, they backed off.

Giving Back: How do you interest people in working for a nonprofit organization?

Bert Berkley: The difference between serving on the Local Investment Commission (the board of directors) and serving on any other civic board is that the Commission makes decisions on where and how money is to be spent. That factor alone allowed a number of civic leaders to agree to serve. Without that unique opportunity for commissioners to decide where money would be spent, a number of

Commission members would never have given their time. The reason volunteers are willing to put in an inordinate amount of time on the Commission and the various LINC committees is that we all believe we are doing something that positively changes the way government works, and, more importantly, changes people's lives for the better.

Giving Back: What corporate executive(s) do you admire most for their contributions (personal and philanthropic)?

Bert Berkley: Those I admire are businesspeople at every rung of the corporate ladder who recognize their responsibility to their community and find time to give back while being successful in their business.

Giving Back: What societal need(s) are you most concerned about?

Bert Berkley: The major problem in the United States is poverty, and the second most important problem is universal health care. It is a disgrace that 36 million Americans live in poverty, and 46.4 million Americans do not have health care insurance.

Giving Back: How can your company become engaged in solutions?

Bert Berkley: Our company foundation supports many good projects on the local and national scene.

Giving Back: What is your personal philosophy that energizes and motivates you?

Bert Berkley: I am energized and motivated by giving back to the community in such a way that people's lives are changed for the better.

Giving Back: How would you measure your success in accomplishing your purpose?

Bert Berkley: LINC has received recognition both nationally and internationally, is helping those that most need help, and I measure my success in the not-for-profit world by the success of LINC.

Notes

1. U.S. Census, "DP-4, Income and Poverty Status in 1989:1990, Geographic Area: Missouri," http://factfinder.census.gov.
2. Missouri State Census Data Center, "1990 Summary Tape File 3 Extract Report: Jackson County," http://oseda.missouri.edu/MOSTATS/Missouri/Counties/xtabs3.Jackson_County_MO.text.
3. U.S. Census statistics, "Poverty Thresholds: 1989," http://www.census.gov/hhes/www/poverty/threshld/thresh89.html

4. U.S. Census, "DP-2, Social Characteristics: 1990, Geographic Area: Missouri," http://factfinder.census.gov.

5. See note 2.

6. U.S. Census statistics (1992), "Cities With 200,000 or More Population Ranked," www.census.gov/ftp/pub/statab/ccdb/ccdb309.txt.

7. "Consolidated Federal Funds Report (CFFR), Fiscal Year 1993," www.census .gov/govs/cffr/93cffmo.txt.

8. "Welfare in 1999: Reform & Reality: Welfare Spending," *Kansas City Star*, www.kcstar.com/projects/welfare/graph9.htm.

9. R. Scott Fosler, "Working Better Together," The Three Sector Initiative: Washington D.C. (2001) pp. 26–27

CHAPTER 3

Changing Lives with Loans from Kiva.org

Give a man a fish and he will eat for a day.
Teach him how to fish and he will feed every day.
Loan him money for a boat and he will have a fishing business.

—OLIVIER OZOUX[1]

For many, giving a donation of cash to an organization that promises to do good things with it is the most common approach to giving back. It's quick, it's easy, and it's immediately satisfying—sort of like those $4 boxes of Girl Scout cookies. Whether putting a few dollars in the collection plate at church, buying a box of Girl Scout cookies, or writing a check to United Way or the Sierra Club or Habitat for Humanity, many nonprofits and charitable organizations indeed have a positive impact on their communities with the money they receive directly from well-meaning donors— and some can have far-reaching impacts on the world as a whole.

However, there is at least one problem with this standard model of giving back: Giving to charities and nonprofit organizations is typically not an interactive event. You write a check and send it, get a thank-you letter (noting your tax-deductible contribution) back in the mail, and that's pretty much the extent of the interaction with the organization, unless you happen to get put on a mailing list for a monthly newsletter or magazine (which you inevitably will). Sure, you get to experience the satisfaction that comes from knowing that you have done good, but this kind of transaction is by nature self-limiting. Once the money is spent by the organization, that's it—it's gone. And you'll no doubt soon receive another appeal to send more money to do more good.

But what if you could find a way to help others that would help them help themselves in a way that not only would give you the immediate satisfaction of giving someone a leg up in their difficult lives, but that might actually enable them to create a self-sustaining way of generating even more money for themselves, their families, and their communities? And what if you received back the money that you donated to this cause—with interest?

This is the idea behind Kiva.org, founded by husband-and-wife team Jessica and Matt Flannery while they were working in Uganda for Village Enterprise Fund. Their idea—microlending (or "person-to-person micro-finance")—is not a new one. It is generally agreed that the idea was put on the map in a big way by Nobel Prize winner Dr. Mohammed Yunus, who founded Grameen Bank. To date, Grameen has given out more than $6 billion in microloans (generally loans in the amount of hundreds or low thousands of dollars) to more than 7 million people in Bangladesh. However, what Jessica and Matt did with the idea was new: creating an online lending platform that allows people in the developed world to loan money to small business owners in the developing world—small business owners who would not typically qualify for conventional busi-ness loans. And although the interest thing is on the back burner for now—a victim of complex U.S. securities laws—when you send your money to Kiva.org, chances are you *will* get your money back, and you can then choose to put it back into your bank account, or loan it to other microentrepreneurs.

Take one look at the Kiva.org Web site and you quickly understand how things work. There's Tran Thi Bay, the owner of a goods distribu-tion business in Soc Son, Vietnam, who has requested a loan of $1,200 to expand her business. So far, Kiva has raised $875 toward the loan. As soon as the entire $1,200 is raised, the loan will be sent to Tran. And there's Akif Quliyev in Baku, Azerbaijan, the owner of an automobile repair business who has requested a loan of $1,100 to buy equipment and raw materials. He has only $25 to go until his loan is funded. Then there's Alicia Francisco, in San Pedro Macoris, Dominican Republic, who sells soft drinks out of a cooler and who needs $800 to buy another cooler and additional equipment to expand her business. At this time, Kiva has raised $700 towards her loan.

When the idea of Kiva.org first began to gel, Jessica had just made the move from working as a staff member in the Public Management Program at the Stanford Business School, to working in Africa for the Village Enterprise Fund (VEF), a nonprofit that makes small grants and loans to businesses in East Africa. Matthew was a software programmer for TiVo, the popular provider of those cool digital video recorders that allow you to zip right through the commercials. Both had grown up in families that sponsored children in Africa through their churches. However, during the course of one of their frequent transoceanic telephone calls, Jessica and Matt had an idea: Instead of sponsoring children, why not sponsor businesses by lending their owners the money they needed to expand operations or buy the supplies or equipment needed to help the business grow?

Indeed, why not?

Says Matt, "Instead of donations, we could focus on loans. This seemed like a dignified, intellectual, and equitable extension that appealed to us at this point in our lives. Instead of benefactor relationships, we could explore partnership relationships. Instead of poverty, we could focus on progress. This was fascinating, not only on a humanitarian level, but it sounded interesting and possibly even fun."

Soon after making this realization, Matt moved to East Africa for a month to be with his wife, to make a short documentary of small business stories, and to see if their idea might make sense. What Matt found was that there were countless small business owners who had a difficult time growing their businesses because they were constantly faced with making decisions about trade-offs in their lives—should they buy medicine for a sick child, or buy more stock for their business? Should they buy food for their hungry family, or use the money to buy seeds and fertilizer for their farm?

Before long, Matt and Jessica were working on a business plan for their new venture for their new organization: Kesho.org ("kesho" in Swahili means *tomorrow*—the name was later changed to Kiva, which means *unity* or *agreement* in Swahili). Excited about their soon-to-be idea, they made the trek to Redmond, Washington, to meet with Geoff Davis, president of Unitus. Unitus is an organization that acts as a microfinance accelerator by combining best practices from the venture capital, investment banking, and strategy consulting industries to help create large-scale, poverty-focused, and commercially sustainable microfinance institutions (MFIs). They presented their ten-page "feasibility plan," which opened thus:

> Through its innovative online platform, Kesho will provide opportunities for people to connect with and invest in individual small-to-medium enterprises (SMEs) in the developing world through soft loans. In doing so, KM aims to alleviate poverty and improve standards of living in developing countries by financially supporting indigenous SMEs.
>
> Kesho will utilize partners within existing microfinance institutions (MFIs) to identity viable SMEs and facilitate the administration of loans. Loan capital will be raised through Kesho's Web site, by offering people the opportunity to contribute to the capital used for a loan to a particular SME—and the opportunity to receive their money back, with a small amount of interest. During the period of a loan agreement, investors will receive frequent, real-time updates on the progress of SMEs working to pay back the loan.
>
> Kesho is currently in the idea stage, but plans to launch a set of pilot microfunds by 01 January 2005.
>
> We are considering plans to operate as a social enterprise with an LLC wing (that will raise investments, facilitate the loan process, and manage Kesho's Web site), and an NGO [nongovernmental organization] wing (that will provide training and operational support to Kesho LLC, and will cover its expenses with tax-deductible donated funds).

Matt and Jessica were certain that they had a great idea, one that would really make a difference for thousands—or maybe even millions—of people in the developing world. To their surprise, however, Geoff was less optimistic that their plan would work. In Geoff's words, "That sounds like it would be hard to scale." And, indeed, after Kiva was founded and started operations, that turned out to be one of the organization's greatest challenges. The problem is that, while it's one thing to connect, track, and administer ten $100,000 loans to entrepreneurs, it's another thing altogether to connect, track, and administer *10,000* $100 microloans. While each of these loan portfolios totals $1 million, the amount of administrative time and energy required to administer the 10,000 microloans far exceeds the ten much larger loans.

But there were other organizational/start-up challenges to consider as well. For one, there was the question of whether to start Kiva as a nonprofit or as for-profit enterprise. When Matt and Jessica were first thinking through their idea, the conventional wisdom was that MFIs would have to be commercialized if they were going to have any significant impact on the developing world—the nonprofit model just wouldn't cut it in the long run. But what impact would this have on potential lenders— average Americans who were looking to give back? (Indeed, a recent survey by Kiva showed that 50% of their current users would not participate in lending if Kiva were a for-profit organization.)

And then there was the legal uncertainty of their model. What kinds of legal and regulatory hoops would Kiva have to jump through to connect lenders in the United States with borrowers around the world? Would Kiva be seen as a bank by regulators, or a securities dealer? Would Kiva be able to make loans (and potentially earn interest on those loans) and still be able to retain its nonprofit, 501(c)(3) status? Would Matt and Jessica find themselves in hot water with the Internal Revenue Service or the U.S. Securities and Exchange Commission (SEC)? And what about the Patriot Act? What if, heaven forbid, a Kiva loan were innocently made to someone who was found to have connections to terrorism? Then what?

There were so many reasons not to start up Kiva.org that Matt and Jessica could have made their lives much simpler by walking away from their idea and getting on with their lives—Matt as a software programmer at TiVo, and Jessica continuing her work in East Africa with the VEF. Indeed, they considered doing just that. But the idea of creating an online lending marketplace was just too compelling, and they continued forward. Soon, they found themselves working late into the night at a series of San Francisco cafes and doughnut shops, designing and building a beta version of the Kiva.org site with the following goals in mind:

- Allow Internet users to make small loans to specific microborrowers around the world, possibly with interest.
- Connect a network of MFIs to our platform and have them post the loan applications of their borrowers to the site.

- Create a financial connection between lender and borrower whereby the lender assumes the default risk.
- Create loans between people, not necessarily organizations, where Kiva acts as a platform and MFIs act as distributors.

Says Matt about their vision for the organization, "We wish to benefit the lenders—people in America, Canada, Europe that are making loans—by connecting them to the lives of people in the developing world. We also wish to benefit low-income entrepreneurs—in over 30 countries now—people that are starting small businesses that are paying for their families, their school fees, and education. They run businesses such as tailoring, fish-selling businesses, clothing businesses—usually in the informal sector. They are usually people who can't access formal banking, who don't have a bank account, who don't usually have a documented identity, and it's mostly women. It turns out women are generally the best people to lend to in the developing world. Finally, a really big part of our mission is to further the cause of the microfinance community in general."

And, with no small amount of persistence and perseverance, Jessica and Matt continued to move forward. Matt made a cold call to the SEC and actually found himself talking with a real live person who offered to help him wade through the sea of regulations. The kiva.org uniform resource locator (URL) was purchased from a cyber squatter for $600, and a logo was designed (by Ryan Pressler—TiVo's visual designer—in trade for a guitar). All that was left was to find some small businesses to feature on the Kiva site. Turning to Moses Onyango—a Ugandan pastor with whom Jessica had worked while in Africa—they were able to find seven businesses in need, and Kiva.org was officially in business.

Kiva.org was designed with the following product philosophy:

- *People are central.* The first thing you notice are faces. Money and organizations are secondary, people are primary.
- *Lending is connecting.* At Kiva.org, lending money is all about information exchange. In a sense, money is a type of information. Lending to someone else creates an ongoing communication between two individuals that is more binding than a donation.
- *Things are always changing.* Every time you load our Web site, it should be different. Every minute, loans are being purchased and

repaid, and stories are being told about the borrowers. This can lead to a dynamic where philanthropy can actually become addictive.

- *Emphasize progress over poverty.* Business is a universal language that can appeal to people of almost every background. This can lead to partnerships rather than benefactor relationships. We appeal to people's interests, not their compassion.
- *Create a data-rich experience.* Whenever it is possible to collect data from the field, we collect it. Over time, we will display as much information about our partners, lenders, and borrowers as possible and let the users decide where money flows.

CASESTUDY

A TYPICAL KIVA.ORG MICROBORROWER

Location: Creel, Chihuahua, Mexico
Business Name: Carmen Xivir Garcia
Activity: Food market
Loan Requested: $925
Repayment Term: 4 months, repaid monthly
Loan Use: Purchase of ingredients

Bernarda is a very hardworking woman. She is married, has three children, and her husband works in construction. Because his wages are not sufficient to cover all the family's needs, Bernarda decided to start her own business making and selling tortillas. Little by little she has expanded her business, reinvesting her profits to increase production. Her family, since they all work together, has been fundamental in the business's growth.

In order to meet her clients demand and expand her business, Bernarda is asking for a $925 loan to purchase the ingredients she needs. She will pay this amount back in just four months. Be a part of this business and improve the lives of Bernarda and her family. They all truly appreciate it.

In April 2005, Matt and Jessica sent an e-mail announcing the site to 300 people on their wedding invitation list. All seven businesses were funded that weekend, raising $3,500. The idea worked! But while this immediate success was intoxicating, Matt and Jessica were faced with an immediate problem: They would need more small businesses seeking loans—*many* more. Without a steady stream of new businesses seeking loans, the site could not sustain itself. While Moses Onyango continued to beat the bushes for more businesses, Matt and Jessica met someone who also had an interest in microfinance: Premal Shah, a PayPal employee who was posting micro-borrower loan applications on eBay (which were quickly being removed by eBay for noncompliance with the site's terms of service).

Says Matt, "We saw Premal as a missing piece of the puzzle. Jessica and I were confessional, careful, thorough, strategic, and technical. Premal was passionate, charismatic, brilliant, wildly enthusiastic, and reckless. That's what we needed to take this organization to the next level." Moses found 50 new qualified borrowers, and Kiva issued its first press release announcing the site. The release failed to generate much attention, and life returned pretty much to normal for Matt and Jessica.

That is, until Kiva.org was featured on the home page of DailyKos, one of the world's most widely read blogs. That same day, all the Kiva loans were sold out, raising $10,000. Even better, the DailyKos mention got the Kiva idea in front of more than a million readers, generating huge amounts of discussion across the Internet—and around the world. That day alone, Matt received almost a thousand e-mail messages from people wanting to know more about Kiva. Many of these messages were from microfinance institutions around the world that wanted to use Kiva.org as a platform for seeking loans for their own portfolios of small business owners. Suddenly, without warning, Kiva.org had hit the big time. After thinking about it over the weekend, Matt quit his job at TiVo to devote himself full time to Kiva.

There were many more challenges along the way, but Matt and Jessica faced them all—and they came out on top. Kiva has achieved its formal objective of alleviating poverty by connecting people through lending, using the best technology available. In the process, the organization has morphed into a technology provider and an online lending marketplace. Today, Kiva has processed more than $8 million cumulative in loans for more than 9,000 small businesses, with a goal of $12 million by the end of 2007. The organization is in the black, and in good financial health. Self-sustainability is critical to Kiva.org, and the organization pays staff salaries and overhead mostly from the "optional fees" that Kiva's lenders voluntarily pay to the organization in addition to the loans they make—normally 10% of the total amount loaned. Kiva has also raised growth capital from a small group of Silicon Valley angel donors, corporate sponsors, and foundations such as the Draper Richards Foundation and the Kellogg Foundation.

Matt and Jessica proved that it doesn't take a lot of money to make a huge impact in the world around you. Armed with a good idea, a lot of drive, and a network of friends, colleagues, and volunteers who were anxious to help, Matt and Jessica have created a self-sustaining organization that has the potential to help millions of people all around the globe, and live on far into the future. And what better legacy is there for anyone to leave in this world?

Q&A WITH MATTHEW FLANNERY, COFOUNDER OF KIVA.ORG (SAN FRANCISCO, CALIFORNIA)

Giving Back: How old were you at the time when you and your wife Jessica founded Kiva.org?

Matthew Flannery: I was 26 when it started.

Giving Back: What gave you the confidence to quit your job at TiVo and make a go of this?

Matthew Flannery: It wasn't necessarily that I had a lot of confidence; it was just that the situation got impractical to do both. When we started the idea, there was so much skepticism from people I knew and also experts in the microfinance field that this idea wasn't something that could spread, it wasn't something that could scale—it's infeasible using the Internet in this way. Can people in these isolated places really use the Internet and can you actually create person-to-person connections this wide reaching? So I sort of believed it, maybe not fully, but I sort of believed a little of the skepticism, at least partially—enough to be really conservative in not dedicating myself to it. And I really didn't believe that other people would find it as interesting as I would. I was really interested in the business stories and interested in following people's businesses in the developing world, and I really liked that connection that comes out of it. I found out, little-by-little, that I wasn't alone and other people wanted to connect to those businesses and be an investor.

Giving Back: Were there people who served as role models for you along the way?

Matthew Flannery: I think there were. I have a really entrepreneurial mind-set so I have always been someone that's dreaming up business ideas. I used to try to come up with one a day—kind of a creative, artistic background. And Jessica came from an international development, poverty-focused perspective so we sort of complimented each other nicely, bringing those two perspectives together. Jessica used to work at World Vision and my sister also used to work at World Vision. They grew up sponsoring children. I went on mission trips with my church when I was young, building houses in Mexico and stuff like that. I really didn't think of it as a career. I just thought of it as something I really cared about. My whole family has always been an international development–focused family. They always had pictures of people in the developing world on the refrigerator that they donated to or sponsored and had that personal connection to.

Giving Back: Were there people along the way that tried to discourage you? How did that impact your efforts?

Matthew Flannery: When you're starting something from scratch, there's a lot of inertia against it. You're fighting the inertia of inactivity, of skepticism, and of vague worries. Although it's very real in your mind, it's hard selling people on your idea, especially when you're coming from somewhere where you don't have a lot of money or reputation. The first thing you encounter is a lot of skepticism. Before I quit my job, I had been working on this idea for one and a half years. I didn't take it that seriously at first, although I kind of secretly took it seriously. On the outside, I would downplay it a lot to protect myself against people's skepticism and criticism. My dad's a CEO of a major company, so he's practical—"Don't quit your job." So you care about something in your heart a lot, and you think about it all the time, but you don't necessarily show that. But really what was happening was that Jessica and I were spending every spare moment working on it in our free time.

Giving Back: What do you think is the most significant contribution you've made to your organization by way of your own personal leadership skills?

Matthew Flannery: I would say having a vision of a product and a service and an idea that was two or three years into the future. So I think where we're at today represents a picture in my mind that I had maybe three years ago, and we're not even there yet. So it's just having a vision of something that's many years ahead and then the dedication to achieve it. We try every day—getting one inch closer to it—building brick by brick, for years and years. It's kind of like coloring in the lines of a picture that you saw. You're painting the colors in a little bit every day, and you have to have the patience to keep at it.

Giving Back: How about financially—did you have to invest a lot of your own money at first?

Matthew Flannery: We didn't have any money to put into it—it was essentially a volunteer effort for years. I think the only real costs we had at first was we were paying someone to upload data from Uganda. Other than that, we had a $20 monthly Web-hosting bill and my time. I gave my guitar to somebody to make the Kiva logo. There were so many hidden costs—taking a business trip some-where, driving somewhere and paying for the gas, but no big major up-front costs were needed. It's just these all these hidden costs and the cost of your time.

Giving Back: Looking back, I know you are not looking back too far, is there anything different you would do or anything you would do differently from your initial approach?

Matthew Flannery: Yes. I would have believed in myself more ear-lier, taken more risks earlier, been more aggressive earlier, and gotten more done earlier. I took a year to think about the idea and to ask questions and get expert advice. If I could go back, I would erase that period and I would have thrown out all the advice I got.

Giving Back: How do you interest volunteers in coming to your organization?

Matthew Flannery: By giving them ownership of something that they are proud of and by showing them transparently the impact they are having. For example, we have a program with 50 translators all over the world who log onto our site, Wikipedia style, and translate the text into different languages. They know that if they didn't translate that text, the person requesting a loan would not get funded, and so they know that their translation is having an effect. I don't have to tell them that it's having an effect, it's not like we give them an award or recognize them. The very fact of the effect of what they're doing day to day shows, it's obvious that they are making an impact. That's the best way, rather than awards or recognizing or compensating people. Actually, if people know in plain view that they are making a difference, they don't need you to motivate them.

Giving Back: Are there any corporate executives that you admire for their personal philanthropic efforts?

Matthew Flannery: Not off the top of my head. I have a lot of mentors and people that have started great companies that I really admire, but I'm not really a philanthropically minded person, if that makes sense. I know that's kind of weird, but I'm more about building businesses and scaling ideas and creatively innovating them. I'm less excited about rich people giving back than I am about creative people building things that benefit the world and making it in a sustainable way, in a way that combines business and social mission. Not to say it's bad to give back, but I think the thing I'm seeing, the thing I'm most interested in participating in, is sustainable businesses. They are not the type of businesses that just make money and then give back. They are the type of businesses that by the very nature of what they do are making a positive impact on the world. There's no binary separation between business and charity; it's a blended approach.

Giving Back: What societal needs are you most concerned about today?

Matthew Flannery: There are so many things to be concerned about. I'm most concerned about exactly what I do, which is giving people access to credit, access to financial systems, the ability to pursue their dreams—connecting people.

Giving Back: What is the personal philosophy that energizes and motivates you?

Matthew Flannery: I think maybe the best word I can think of is *surrender*—surrendering yourself to something greater than yourself. That's a little vague, but that's sort of the rallying cry of my business—just training yourself to a bigger cause and not worrying about what you can't control, but worrying about exactly what you can control every day. So when I say surrender, like surrendering your fears, and when I say my biggest regret is waiting a year to start the business, I think that was because I had a lot of fear. So I was able to personally surrender that to something larger, which was a real empowering moment. I started to try to live that lesson in my daily life every day and make up for lost time.

Giving Back: How do you measure your success in achieving your business goals?

Matthew Flannery: There are a lot of different metrics. There's the number of users on our site, which today is at approximately 80,000. That's the most important metric for our business—user base. There's also loan volume. We sent about $7.9 million to small business owners in the developing world. In a couple of days, it will be $8 million. So there's that. There are a lot of qualitative things that are harder to track, like the quality of the stories on the site and the number of amazing life-changing things we hear from people involved with Kiva—both in the United States and abroad. But the most quantitative metrics are number of users, number of dollars, and also delinquency rate and repayment rate.

Giving Back: How do you measure your success in achieving your personal goals?

Matthew Flannery: The financial health of the organization is paramount—the burn rate, income, financial sustainability—and then there are qualitative things like the general morale and the happiness of everyone I work with. That's a little bit harder to gauge, but you can get an idea from it.

Note

1. http://www.ozoux.com/eclectic/archive/2006/03/18/kiva-charitable-loans.

CHAPTER 4

The Wizard Oz, UPS, and Annie E. Casey

We must help others to help ourselves. Our horizon is as distant as our mind's eye wishes it to be.

—JIM CASEY, FOUNDER, UPS[1]

Hear the letters *UPS,* and chances are the first thing that comes to mind might be that big, brown truck that drives down your street dropping off a never-ending supply of packages along the way. Or maybe you'll think about the UPS driver—in the company's ubiquitous brown uniform—who drops by your office to pick up the boxes waiting in reception. But, perhaps the last thing you think of when you hear *UPS* is a company that is deeply committed to giving back to the communities in which it does business. However, with a multitude of volunteer and philanthropic activities for employees to choose from (in 2006 alone, more than 23,000 UPS employees in over 50 countries donated more than 154,000 hours of service to their local communities),[2] this would be a deeply mistaken impression.

UPS has a long history of social involvement—a history in which the company's employees take great pride. UPS was founded—as a bicycle messenger service, originally named American Messenger Company—in 1907 by high school dropout Jim Casey. Casey was a low-key, self-effacing man who was dedicated to his company's customers, its people, and the communities in which UPS did business. And, when it came to giving back, Casey set the bar very high. During the course of his many years at the helm of the company, he and his brother gave most of the money they earned—more than $438 million—to the Annie E. Casey Foundation, which they founded in memory of their mother. The Foundation's mission is *to foster public policies, human-service reforms, and community supports that more effectively meet the needs of today's vulnerable children and families.*

But more than giving money to the causes he believed in, Jim Casey created a culture of giving at UPS, and he set an example for the leaders who followed in his footsteps. One of these leaders, Oz Nelson—who worked his way up the ladder from customer service representative to chairman and CEO of UPS—helped continue the company's track record of success, both in business and in giving back. During his time at the helm of UPS, Nelson virtually doubled the company's revenues—from $12.3 billion in 1989 to $22.2 billion in 1996—while its profit surged from $693 million to $1.1 billion during the same period.[3]

And when it came to giving back, Oz didn't just try to reach the bar that Jim Casey had set so high—he leapt right over it. The first in his family to earn a college degree, Oz cofounded and chaired the Kentucky Partnership for Schools, a nonprofit organization dedicated to improving education for all of Kentucky's students. He served on Georgia Governor Roy Barnes's Education Reform Study Commission, and headed a $90 million fund-raising campaign for his alma mater, Ball State University in Indiana. Not only that, but Oz has served as national director of the United Way of America and chairman of the Annie E. Casey Foundation; he succeeded Home Depot cofounder Bernard Marcus as chairman of the Centers for Disease Control and Prevention (CDC) Foundation; and he serves on the board of trustees for the Carter Center, where he is cochairing a $150 million fund-raising campaign. In his spare time, Oz has been active in the Metro Atlanta Chamber of Commerce, where he chaired the organization's education committee. Long story short—if there were a gold medal for giving back, Oz surely would have won it many times over.

But when Oz was growing up and thinking about the life stretching out before him, he didn't plan for things to turn out this way. When he was in college, he had no big dreams of giving back, nor did he have any idea that he would someday lead what is today a major package-delivery company, with some 15.6 million packages and documents delivered each business day throughout the United States and to more than 200 countries and territories around the world, and with annual revenues of more than $47 billion.[4] In fact, it was really a matter of chance that he ended up working at UPS at all.

Says Oz, "I got a phone call one day at my frat house at Ball State University from someone at UPS. One of my fraternity brothers worked for UPS, and I knew a little bit about the company from him. I had been impressed with what he told me about them. When I mentioned to my father—who managed a factory in my hometown of Kokomo, Indiana—that I had a friend working at UPS, he said, 'Boy I don't know much about them, but they have got the hardest-working driver I've ever seen in my life delivering to our factory. Find out how they do that.' So my father was impressed, too.

"So I got the phone call, and the UPS man said he knew I was a business major, and he asked, 'Do you have a job yet?' I told him, 'No,' and he asked, 'How would you like to interview at UPS?' I thought about it for a minute, and I said, 'Well, I'd love to talk to you about it.' I graduated about a week after that—in 1959—and I went to UPS for the interview. The interviewer said, 'I guess you're a good friend of Lou and Charlie's,' and I said, 'Yes I am.' He then said, 'Well, if you're half the man they are, we want you. You've got a job.' That was the interview, and I accepted the job before I even knew what the salary was because I was favorably impressed with the company."

So Oz went to work for UPS as a salesman–customer service representative. In those days, UPS employees did a little bit of everything, so a typical day for Oz wasn't limited to just sales and customer service; it included delivering packages, washing trucks when they needed it, and moving them around the parking lot in the evenings if they needed that—whatever it took to keep things going smoothly. As a result, Oz had the opportunity to see many different aspects of the business and what worked—and what didn't.

After a year with UPS, Oz went into the armed forces for six months. After his tour of duty ended, Oz went right back to work for UPS. Eventually, his UPS sales territory changed from Kokomo to South Bend, Indiana, and he worked his way up the ladder, becoming a supervisor of sales and customer service representatives, and then he was put in charge of an entire district, then the region, and eventually the national sales and service operation. UPS is a promote-from-within company, so virtually everyone is hired at the lowest level and works their way up through the organization to the extent they want and are able to.

Over a period of about 20 years, Oz moved through a variety of positions in Indiana, to Chicago, and then to the national office in New York. After that, he helped to open UPS's first foreign operations—in Germany—and then returned to the United States, where he became the national customer service manager with responsibilities for a number of areas, including advertising, public relations, and marketing. Interestingly enough, in UPS's first 65 years of life, it had never had a marketing department. So Oz created UPS's first marketing department. He later became the company's chief financial officer (CFO), although Oz himself admits that he didn't have a day's training in finance. Recalls Oz, "At our first board meeting after I had been made CFO, I recall one of our outside directors coming up to me, saying, 'Oz, just what exactly are your qualifications to be CFO of this company?' I thought for a minute and I said, 'Well, the only thing I can think of is my wife's got an accounting degree.' He laughed and said, 'Great, she can check your work when you take it home at night.'"

While Oz served as UPS's CFO, there was a technology revolution going on in the shipping business. Shipping upstart FedEx had discovered that while customers loved to have their letters and packages delivered overnight, they perhaps loved even more FedEx's ability to provide package tracking information along the way. This, however, took a lot of computer horsepower to accomplish—something UPS had not yet committed to. However, the company soon saw the writing on the wall, and Oz was tapped to take over UPS's entire computer and information technology operation. In 1986, Oz directed a $2 billion, five-year technology upgrade program with the goal of tracking packages more quickly and accurately, and turning mountains of customer and package information into a marketing tool. The longer-term goal was to use technology to improve package sorting and delivery operations.

After serving as the company's CFO, Oz was promoted to chairman and CEO, positions he occupied for seven years, from 1989 through 1996. All in all, Oz was an employee at UPS for more than 37 years. After stepping down from his position as chairman and CEO, he remained on the board for another five years. During much of his career at UPS—and after he left the company—Oz Nelson found many different ways to use his business experience to help nonprofit organizations. Traditionally, nonprofits have avoided adopting the kind of strict metrics and accountability that Fortune 500 businesses like UPS do as a matter of course—they sometimes get caught up thinking about processes and activities instead of results. However, by attracting talented businesspeople onto their boards, or into top leadership positions, nonprofits can often become more efficient operationally, and more effective in achieving their goals.

This was the case at the United Way, where Oz served as national director for a number of years. During his tenure there, he helped change the organization's focus on processes and activities to a new focus on results. This was a breakthrough both for the United Way and for Oz Nelson, who witnessed firsthand the positive impact his business skills could have on a nonprofit organization. In addition, the United Way offered Oz an opportunity to get UPS employees involved in giving back to their community.

Says Oz, "United Way was a vehicle that we could use within our corporation to get our people more involved. Early on, we actually had a policy that said there will be no solicitation in the company—we thought it would be improper for people to go to their employees or people that might work for them and suggest that they give money to anything. We thought they should do that voluntarily, on their own. However, our chairman at the time—a fellow by the name of George Lamb, who I just revered—told me one day, 'You know, Oz, we have this policy against soliciting for nonprofits. I think its intent is good, but I have been talking to a lot of our people who have become fairly well off now as our company has grown and prospered. I asked them what they're doing and I've been disappointed with some of the answers I've heard. I'm beginning to think we're wrong—I think we should do something that would encourage our people to get more involved both personally and financially in helping those people that need help.' We already had a number of programs at UPS, including the Better Boys Foundation in Chicago, and several minority organizations that we thought were effective, but George wanted to go beyond that. He asked me what I thought about it and I said I agree and, in fact, I think I am guilty of not doing as much as I can and should be doing."

So George Lamb decided that the United Way was what the company should focus its efforts on, and he asked Oz to help him get the company involved. Today, UPS is the world's largest giver to the United

Way, and the company's employees—and the company itself—gave close to $60 million to the United Way in 2006. However, there is more to the relationship between the United Way and UPS employees. There is also a strong sense and tradition of volunteerism. UPS has a huge neighbor-to-neighbor program that fosters volunteerism with the United Way, the agencies they support, and others. In turn, the United Way has had a positive impact on UPS—the pride that employees feel for being part of a company that supports good things like the United Way can't be bought with any amount of money. It was a gift that gave back to the company in ways that they had never even expected. Says Oz, "I used to travel around the country visiting CEOs of major companies and talking to them about ways that they could improve and strengthen the United Way programs in all their locations throughout the country—and even out of the country in some cases."

As Oz traveled the countryside talking to CEOs each year during fund-raising campaigns, he began to be concerned that thanking the CEO for the great job they did last year, but then asking them to come up with even more money the next year was not really solving the problem. Says Oz, "I would go in and see this CEO and thank them for the great job they did for the United Way—and how much money they gave and their superb example of volunteerism. I gave them examples of things that were bettered because of what they had done. At the end of the presentation, I would say, 'But you know the problem—we even need more money, the problems are worse. I got to thinking, 20 years from now, is this going to be the same message the United Way brings? When are we going to start saying, 'Here are some problems we've solved, and things are actually getting better?'" Oz, therefore, pushed for the development of a national strategic plan for the United Way.

The United Way has about 1,400 chapters around the country, each with an independent board of directors, so there is a fair amount of autonomy within the organization and each chapter works directly with its local nonprofits, agencies, and other community-based organizations. Back when Oz started working with the United Way, many local organizations that the charity worked with were more concerned about making payrolls, keeping enough money available for operations, and counting how many people they served, than about whether their organizations were really delivering the results that they should.

Oz was convinced that there were real solutions out there if people set the solutions as goals—not just feeding more people or just serving more people. For Oz, it was all about getting people on their feet and helping them take care of themselves, so he pushed the United Way to aim a lot of their programs in exactly that direction. Because of Oz's background at UPS—a company where results are *everything*—he was able to help the United Way teach its local chapters how to work with organizations locally to make them more able to deliver results that will make a real difference in their communities. Because of this kind of training to United Way chapters, the organization has helped change the mind-set of thousands of nonprofits around the United States over the past several years.

And then there was the Annie E. Casey Foundation. Oz had long felt that there was a huge amount of money being spent nationally by the U.S. government and others trying to help poor children and their families, and it was frankly being used poorly. The objective at Annie E. Casey was to be a little different. There was a definite feeling that the solution to poverty was not just asking the government and donors for money—over and over again. Instead, the Foundation believed that one of its key goals should be unearthing best practices and shifting the money that was being spent on things that weren't delivering their promise to things that actually made a difference. According to Oz, "Annie E. Casey has more measurements and goals than you can shake a stick at, and they have delivered some incredible results over the years. They have a sub-stantial budget that is the result of a gift by Jim Casey of UPS stock that has grown to over $3 billion in value. We were able to spend in the neighborhood of $240 million a year on various projects—all aimed at helping disadvantaged children and their families—which was another area that was important to me."

For Oz Nelson, giving back was something that people should make an everyday part of their lives. At Ball State, he was very active in his fraternity—Sigma Phi Epsilon—which was involved in many community projects. He even cochaired the Campus Chest Campaign. At UPS, Jim Casey set very high standards of conduct and ethics that were extensively preached and followed throughout the organization. Back in the 1960s—during the time of the Civil Rights movement—the company's human resources department worked hard to hire minorities and ensure that fair promotional standards were put in place. For Jim Casey—and for the company—it was simply the right thing to do.

But just because something was the right thing to do didn't mean that it was the easy thing to do. When Oz became CEO of UPS, George Lamb came to Oz and said, "I'm going to tell you something that served me well as CEO and you may want to think about, but there will be times when you will have some very difficult decisions to make. Some will be really trying and you will really ponder what the right thing to do is. I have a simple test I put those kinds of hard questions to and if you will consider it, it may serve you well, too. The test is this: If that decision that I made were printed on the front page of my hometown newspaper, would I be proud of it?" More than a few times, Oz used this test to ensure that the decisions he made were the right ones.

For any business, there is a balance between doing what's best for the company—which often translates into making as much money as possible—and doing what's best for the customer. For Oz Nelson, it was all about providing the best service he could to his customers at a fair price. Says Oz, "We could have, frankly, made a lot more money had we wanted to. People would have paid a higher price, but I never believed in charging as much as the buyer would pay, and that was not our practice— we didn't believe in that. Jim Casey preached to us to give our customers more than they expect, never less. So I was very, very interested and driven to maintain the highest service levels possible and do more for customers. There's always this supposed trade-off that you hear from folks: What do you want—production or service? We never gave them a simple answer to that, because the correct answer is 'Both.' As we went around the country and looked at our best service areas, it turned out that the production was the best, too. Our employees in our best areas were simply paying attention to the little details of the job—all of them—and doing them well."

Although Oz Nelson has left behind a remarkable career with UPS, his real legacy may be the stamp he has left on the nonprofits, the foundations, and the community-based organizations with which he has worked. Oz is clearly motivated by a drive to help solve our nation's social ills. But the question remains: How do you motivate others to join in with their own expertise, time, and energy. For Oz, the answer is simple: "I have found that there are lots of people who would do a lot more if they were given the opportunity and maybe a little bit of a nudge. In Atlanta, you can get volunteers in huge numbers for just about anything. The challenge is to make that anything important so they will stay with it. Make it fulfilling and have it make a difference so it's worthwhile. There are a lot of nonprofits out there that are simply going through the motions, in my mind, and there are a lot of them doing great work. We've got to get them all doing great work. There's so much replication of effort out there among nonprofits—we've got way too many, in my opinion, and it's hard to keep track of them anymore."

And Oz is still driven by the issues he is personally passionate about. Today, one such issue is keeping kids out of jail. Says Oz: "There are places in this nation where they're closing down jails, and there are other places in this nation where they can't build them fast enough. So what's the difference? The places where they're closing down the jails have figured out how they can keep kids out of jail. They have programs in place to keep them from recommitting crimes, which means they can spend a whole lot less money on building these places to store them where they learn bad things. That doesn't mean there aren't some juveniles that should be in jail—there are. But I can show you places in this nation where the number of incarcerated juveniles has been reduced by 40 to 45% and the recidivism is less than it was to start with. They can do this because they're getting the right kind of support back in their neighborhoods, they've gotten follow-up training, and they are doing a better job of identifying which kids really have serious problems and which ones don't. Judges are being given alternatives that make sense instead of putting them in jail because they can't figure out what else to do with them. It doesn't take a lot of common sense, but it does take some."

Oz continues, "When you talk to a potential volunteer and tell them that story about the success places are having keeping youths out of jail, for example, it's easy to pull them in. They'll say, 'Yeah, I'd like to help do that. I don't want to see kids put in jail that shouldn't be in jail; I want them to be successful.' An issue that particularly bugs me is putting children—or their parents—in jails far removed from their homes. It makes family visits almost impossible. We should be encouraging family relationships during such trying times to stimulate the possibility of successful family reformation after release. Just picture a wife and three young children living in Chattanooga, Tennessee with the husband (and father) serving a sentence in a Northern Kentucky rural penitentiary. There is no public transportation to such places. How can this family sustain a relationship? What long-term effect does it have on the children? The spouse? As far as the children are concerned, the father returning home is a virtual stranger to them."

But jail and its impact on children is just one issue Oz is concerned about. Says Oz, "There are just so many things out there that don't make sense, like splitting up families in foster care. Half the homeless in this country come through the foster care system; and in one of our foundations, The Jim Casey Youth Opportunity Initiative, we are doing a whole lot of work to reduce the number of homeless young people, and we're making progress. We're spending about $4 to $5 million a year right now through a couple of foundations we're working with, and it's working. Those kids are starting to catch on, but at 18 years old, if your children were turned out, maybe no job, maybe no place to stay, what do you think would happen to them? And if you set them up in an apartment and they have a job and they get laid off three months later, what do you think happens to them? That's what we're trying to fix, and we're scoring in several places now around the country. But people hear these stories, and they say, 'Gee, that's not right, what can we do about it?' Then it's easy to get good people to volunteer."

Clearly, Oz Nelson is not planning to stop giving back anytime soon. In fact, spend some time with him, and you'll likely come to the conclusion that he's just getting started. And you'll probably want to know what you can do to help.

Q&A with Oz Nelson, Former Chairman and CEO of UPS (Atlanta, Georgia)

Giving Back: What societal needs were you most concerned about when you were at UPS?

Oz Nelson: I would say that one thing UPS made me more aware of was the unequal treatment of people of color in the country, and UPS was one of the very early leaders in being aware of that and trying to do something about it. I still laugh at some of our early steps, but we certainly, I think, led our industry in becoming a company that was blind to color. We worked with policies on that, of course, and I brought it to all the organizations I worked in. I served on a number of boards and I brought that mind-set with me even to corporate boards, as well as the nonprofits and others, to make sure we had what I considered to be the right representation to be effective, and to gain from that kind of a diversity of experiences and backgrounds. So that's one area. Another area is disadvantaged children, and I had an interest in that for some time. The founder of UPS, Jim Casey, set up a foundation to address the problems of foster children, of which I was fortunate enough to become a board member and then later chaired it for about 10 to 12 years.

My years with the Annie E. Casey Foundation gave me time and information to understand how serious the problems were in not-for-profits, gave me the opportunity to think of some of the managerial and strategic skills that we had at UPS that I could apply to the nonprofit world, along with the help of others. I was, frankly, amazed at how much could be added to the work that was being done by doing what we considered the basics at UPS in terms of accountability and planning, work measurement and goal setting, benchmarking, and all the kinds of things that had kind of become second nature to us at UPS.

Giving Back: Were there people who served as role models for you personally on the way as you were growing up to giving back to the community?

Oz Nelson: Well, my mother was the one that probably set the best example for me. I can't remember my father doing anything but working. He put in a lot of hours, and I don't remember him doing anything other than trying to take care of the family and coming to an occasional sporting event that my brother and I participated in. My mother was president of the PTA at the school. My mother volunteered as a Cub Scout den leader when my brother and I were going through school. She volunteered for a number of different things, and she set a very good example for me. She really cared about people and talked about it, and I attribute a lot of my awareness to good things being done by volunteers to observing and listening to her. She helped a lot.

Giving Back: Were there people along the way who tried to discourage you from these different things you were working in, these different areas?

Oz Nelson: I have a lot of interests, and I have trouble probably focusing as much as I should sometimes because I get involved with a lot of things. I can recall an outside director sitting down with me one time and saying, "Oz, you do some great stuff here, and the company's going fine, but you really spend a lot of time on some of these other things and I'm worried about it a little bit. Something might get by you, and maybe you should consider cutting some of these outside activities a little bit." I thought for a while and I said, "I appreciate your coming and telling me that because I know you mean it, and I have a lot of respect for you and even more now that you have come to discuss this with me." I said, "I will give it some thought, but my initial reaction is that I am not going to change. You tell me there's something that we need to be doing and it's not getting the right attention; I will make sure it gets the right attention. I'll pay attention to what is needed, but I really think these other things are important, not only to the company, but to the country at large, for example, education reform."

I was doing a lot of work in education reform and I was flying back and forth to Kentucky from our corporate offices. I chaired the Kentucky Partnership for School Reform for six years, and it took a fair amount of time and the United Way took quite a bit of time. We were trying to really accomplish quite a lot there, and my partners at UPS loved it and supported it, thought it was important.

We were fortunate because of promotion from within. We had a tremendous amount of depth in almost every job, and when I stepped out as CEO, I honestly could have named 7 or 8 people who could have replaced me. We picked the one I thought was best, but I can tell you 7 or 8 people were capable of stepping in. They had the right kind of experiences and successes and 20, 30 years of promotions and working in various places and various jobs, and that gave us some flexibility to do more.

Giving Back: What do you think is the most significant contributions that you've made organizationally by way of your own personal leadership skills?

Oz Nelson: I think what I brought to nonprofits was, first of all, a lot of respect for people who do that work, and second, teaching them a way to think about how they could be more effective by giving others credit and thinking about what the problem is, and how it could be solved. What does it take to find a solution, and what are we doing now that isn't working? What are you frustrated with, and is anybody out there doing it better? Are we looking at best practices and benchmarking and bringing all those things that are practiced at UPS and other places to nonprofits, and encouraging them to do the same?

There are great nonprofit leaders out there and some of them are shooting the lights out, in my opinion, in their areas, and they have picked up best practices just as business has. We were not good at some of these things, either. We were stuck with silos, the same as some of the nonprofits are. I have seen it in government work. I have done a lot of work with the CDC, and we are trying to transform the CDC into a service-oriented organization, and we are making some progress, I think. It's goal setting and team building and thinking how we can make things better.

Giving Back: Looking back, would you take a different approach to these different things?

Oz Nelson: What I do when I get with an organization is to find out when they last did a strategic plan—and usually it's too long ago—and start thinking about how we can get a few people together and start thinking about how we're doing and what our biggest challenges are, and maybe new ways and old ways and best ways to make things better. I have worked on strategic plans at the Carter Center and at the CDC, the CDC Foundation, United Way locally, United Way nationally, and a number of organizations like Ball State University and Ball State University Foundation. When people start concentrating on what we're really trying to do and how we can do it better, and they stop thinking of how they go about just doing more of the same over and over again, it creates a whole different atmosphere. If you let them develop the plan and you don't do it for them, it's a plan that they believe in and they can make work. I remember at the CDC early on, about three or four years ago, we sat down with those folks and said, "Who are the CDC's customers?", and, boy, we got answers, and this is with their upper management group. We got answers, such as the president of the United States, the Senate, Congress, the head of Health and Human Services, the state public health agencies, on and on, and we got all through this exercise and we finally pretty much uniformly said, "Gee, the customer is the United States citizen." "So everything you do should be aimed at improving the health of the United States citizens," and we said, "Well, who are all these people you mentioned?", and we decided they were partners. They were people who could help. It's a basic exercise we go through. We've gone through it for years in lots of places, but for a government agency it was a revelation and we started changing things. Dr. Gerberding is driving it and driving it, and she has had a lot of grief from it, but she's making steady progress. Constructive dialogue changes things.

Giving Back: What personal philosophy energizes and motivates you?

Oz Nelson: I hate to see people taken advantage of, and I hate to see classes of people, groups of people, not get the opportunity to be successful. These inequities bug me, and that's why I have trouble focusing and have trouble saying no to things, although I am getting a lot better at it now that I'm 70.

Giving Back: Earlier, we asked you what societal needs you were concerned about when you were at UPS. Are there things today that are particularly troubling to you?

Oz Nelson: Yes, I am really concerned about all the people being incarcerated and, in fact, when you look at black people, a huge number of males and an increasing numbers of females are in jail, and they come out and people won't hire them. I'm familiar with a program in Indianapolis. I met with the mayor, and our foundation has put in some money and some consultants to help them. I went into this one area and I was talking to one of the workers there and I said, "What do you do with people who are coming out of prison?" and this is the first time I ever heard this answer. She said, "Well, the next one coming out," and this was in November, "will be in February. His name is John such and such. He's been in for two and a half years for such and such. He's going to move into this house at this address with this relative. So–and–so has agreed to give him a job, and he has this person who will be his sponsor to work with him to help him stay on the straight and narrow." That's what needs to be done, and it can be done, and there are all sorts of businessmen in this country who won't hire someone with a record until you sit and talk to them and tell them what the problem is, how many of them there are, and what's going to happen and then they start saying, "Well, gee, maybe I could do something about that." Nobody's ever sat down and talked to them about it and that bothers me a lot, and, also, I have a friend who runs an organization that works with children of imprisoned parents and I think they are doing wonderful work. I think there's not much more you can do for imprisoned parents than to keep them close to their kids, and make them want to come out and take care of them. I think that's a real plus and work needs to be done in that area. That's a newer area that I've gotten very involved in during the past two years, and I'm very active in this foster care thing, trying to help kids transition out of foster care into self-reliance and being able to take care of themselves.

Giving Back: How do you measure your success in achieving your goals both in business and personally?

Oz Nelson: Well, for example, in Annie Casey, the work we do there and in Jim Casey, those two foundations, we have very precise goals and we know exactly where we started. We know how much improvement we've got and we know exactly how much more we need to get, and we have put in place the things that need to be done to get them, and if we don't get those goals, then we change the practices. I can tell you that's the way with everything that we try to do at Casey. We spend, probably at one time it was as high as 15%, now it's more like 8% or 9% on measurement. That's a lot of money, but if you don't know where you are to start with and you don't know what's possible, how do you measure where you ought to be? We have gotten awfully good at that at Jim Casey and at Annie Casey, and I can tell you UPS is excellent at it, and that's where I learned it. You can walk into any operating center at UPS and ask them about production and service and cost, as well as how they're doing with their United Way campaign. All those things are measured. They know exactly what they want to get, and they know how they're going to get there, and they're making progress or they're in the process of changing what they're doing so they will make progress. That's what you have to do and the United Way is the same thing here in Atlanta. We have set goals on everything we're working on. We're making real progress on the homeless and we're going to make a lot more. When I worked in education, we had lots of goals set up. Kentucky moved from about 43rd to about 33rd in the nation in that six-year period, and they still continue to gain. All these things are possible with strategic thinking and planning and goal setting. These activities make for success.

NOTES

1. www.casad.org/Hum2000intro/Resources1.htm.
2. www.sustainability.ups.com/social/community/foundation.html.
3. Roger Donway, "The Fioretti of Self-Fulfillment," www.objectivistcenter.org/cth–102-The_Fioretti_Self_Fulfillment.aspx.
4. Hoovers.com (accessed August 21, 2007).

CHAPTER 5

The Future's Bright
for Boston Kids

*Visions describe what best should be, could be—if and when mankind
has the will to make them real.*

—JAMES ROUSE

W hen Linda Mason and Roger Brown met for the first time at the
Yale School of Management in the late 1970s, there's a good chance
that they didn't imagine that one day they would together found the nation's
largest worksite child care company. And it's also not likely that they imag-
ined that they would one day start up one of the country's most effective
nonprofits dedicated to serving the needs of homeless children. In fact, they
probably didn't even have an inkling that, by 1987, they would be married
and well on the way to a lifetime of making a difference in the lives of
thousands of people. But these things have all come true—and much more.

Although it was founded little more than 20 years ago—in 1986—
Bright Horizons Family Solutions has grown quickly to become the largest provider of corporate-sponsored child care and early education in the
world. The company currently has more than 18,000 employees working
in 41 states around the country (and in the District of Columbia, Puerto
Rico, Canada, the United Kingdom, and Ireland) with annual revenues
at around $700 million. Bright Horizons serves more than 600 clients,
including 90 Fortune 500 companies and 65 of *Working Mother* magazine's

"100 Best Companies for Working Mothers," and is the only child care company listed in *Fortune* magazine's "100 Best Companies to Work for in America."

The company's mission is to provide innovative programs that help children, families, and employers work together to be their very best. Bright Horizons Family Solutions operates full-service child care and early education centers in companies such as Motorola, Starbucks, Johnson & Johnson, and Citigroup. The company also offers before- and after-school and vacation care, summer camps, and college admissions counseling services. In recent years, the company has also begun expanding its offerings into private and charter elementary schools.

As if founding the nation's largest provider of corporate-sponsored child care and early education in the United States weren't enough, in 1988 Linda Mason and Roger Brown founded a nonprofit organization: Horizons for Homeless Children. Every week, this organization touches the lives of more than 2,000 Massachusetts homeless children through Playspaces (educational and recreational spaces) in shelters and provides childcare for 175 children through its three Community Children's Centers, Boston's only comprehensive, full-time early education and child care centers specifically for homeless children.

But we are getting ahead of ourselves. Before there was Bright Horizons Family Solutions, and before there was Horizons for Homeless Children, there were just Linda Mason and Roger Brown, whose separate paths through life led them to meet one another—at the right place, and at the right time.

Roger grew up in the South during the height of the Civil Rights movement and had witnessed the forced desegregation of his school, which left quite an impression on him. Says Brown, "Living through school desegregation in the South and the bitter racism it exposed influenced my life profoundly. It taught me that adults could sometimes be very mistaken. Fortunately, my parents were not in that group."[1] Brown eventually enrolled in the physics program at North Carolina's Davidson College. During his senior year, he attended a presentation made by a representative recruiting math teachers for a small school in Kenya. Roger signed on for a year, living in a hut without running water or electricity—in the same conditions as his students and their families.

It was during this time that Roger decided that after he finished his teaching commitment in Africa, he would enroll in graduate school to study management and leadership with a focus on international development. It was at Yale that he met Linda Mason—a classical pianist who had studied at the Rachmaninov Conservatory in Paris, and who shared Roger's interest in international development—so much so that they got summer jobs working together on the Cambodia-Thailand border, running Land Bridge, a food relief program for CARE and UNICEF that served up to 25,000 starving people a day.

After graduating from Yale, Linda and Roger accepted management consulting positions—Linda at Booz, Allen, and Roger at Bain & Company. They continued in management consulting positions until the end of 1984, when they were invited to join Save the Children Federation as co-country directors with the goal of establishing a brand-new famine relief program in Sudan. During their year-and-a-half stay in Khartoum, Linda and Roger built Save the Children's largest relief program—serving more than 400,000 people with an annual operating budget of $14 million.

After building a large, successful relief organization in Sudan, Linda and Roger decided in the summer of 1986 to return to the United States. However, they didn't know exactly what they wanted to do with themselves. Although each had worked for consulting firms before moving to Africa, they both knew that they wanted to do something entrepreneurial— to create an organization that would make an impact on people. Because most of their previous work experience had been with children, that's where they first focused their efforts.

Says Linda Mason, "My husband, Roger Brown, and I had just come back from Africa. The work we had done in East Africa was very entrepreneurial. Save the Children Federation gave us a couple million dollars of start-up capital that they had raised for African relief, yet they had no operation on the ground. So we went over with a couple million dollars, with the expectation that we would raise significantly more, and it was in the midst of that African famine, so it was quite a crisis. We quickly went around the country, figured out where the needs were greatest, where we could intervene, and then started an organization that grew to be quite large."[2]

Back in the States, as they looked further into entrepreneurial possibilities, some statistics struck them. In the mid-1980s, the United States had experienced a momentous demographic change as a result of large numbers of women—specifically, mothers—entering the workforce. In fact, in 1986, 60 percent of all mothers with children under the age of five were working full time. Just a decade earlier, in the 1970s, the percentage of mothers with children under the age of five stood at just 18 percent. This increase indicated that there was a dramatic increase in the need for child care in the United States from the 1970s to the 1980s. At the same time, Linda and Roger discovered that the number of child care facilities had grown only about 3 percent a year, far less than the increase in demand. In addition, many of the child care services that did exist were of low quality. So, the answer was obvious: The future was to meet this growing need by providing high-quality child care services. To put the icing on their idea, Linda and Roger also decided that companies would be able to attract and retain good employees by providing child care at their worksites, so they would certainly be interested in working with a company that could provide on-site services.

This idea became Bright Horizons, founded by Linda Mason and Roger Brown in 1986. After further reviewing the data, and creating a business plan, Linda and Roger were able to quickly secure an initial $2 million in funding from Bain Capital and other venture capitalists to commence operations. However, as it turned out, Bright Horizons was ahead of its time—*far* ahead of its time. As pioneers in the move to provide child care at company worksites—less than 3 percent of child care was being provided on client premises when Bright Horizons began operations in the late 1980s—the idea was initially met with widespread indifference. The question executives asked was, "Why should we provide child care to our employees—in our facilities—when it's the parents' job to do that?"

Says Linda Mason, "So, it was a huge struggle the first several years— maybe four or five years—while we really weren't sure if we could get the concept off the ground. What saved us was that we firmly believed in the idea; we just thought, 'It's got to work.' We never gave up against all sorts of reasons why we should. But we knew it would have to take off, because we just thought, 'How can companies hire and keep good workers if they have no child care for their children?'"

It actually took about five years for the idea to catch on—five very difficult years for Linda and Roger, as they questioned their idea and wondered if they had made the right decision. In response to the collective corporate shrug that greeted them, they decided to change their pitch. Instead of focusing on directly selling their idea to companies, they decided to try selling to the real estate developers who were building office park after office park in the Boston suburbs for these same companies to move into. The 1980s was a boom time in the Boston area, which—with its Route 128 corridor—was widely considered to be the Silicon Valley of the East. As it turned out, commercial real estate developers had overbuilt in the area, which made it more difficult to attract tenants while maintaining prices that would earn them a profit. Long story short—Linda and Roger found success selling developers on the idea of providing prospective tenants with on-site child care as a perk. And once they found success selling the idea to developers—and got their operations off the ground—they started finding success selling the idea directly to companies.

By 1997, Bright Horizons had grown to 150 centers, serving about 20,000 children. However, the initial group of venture capitalists—the people and firms who had funded the company's start-up a little more than 10 years earlier—were getting restless. They wanted to cash out their investments and move on. This meant that Bright Horizons would need to find a way to raise the cash necessary to buy out the venture capitalist's investments. The solution? Go public. So, in 1997, Bright Horizons became a publicly traded company and, in 1998, it merged with its largest competitor—Nashville-based Corporate Family Solutions, creating a new company: Bright Horizons Family Solutions.

One of the lessons from working with Save the Children that Linda Mason and Roger Brown took with them when they founded Bright Horizons was that every dollar counts. Reflecting back on her experience helping to feed hundreds of thousands of victims of war and famine in Sudan, Mason says, "Most refugee operations are horribly run. There was high turnover. At best, there's a lot of wastage, and at worst, there's a terrible lost opportunity." And these were mistakes that Mason and Brown were committed to not making when they formed their own nonprofit organization—Horizons for Homeless Children—in 1988, and then the Bright Horizons Foundation for Children in 1999.

The tragedy of homelessness is pervasive in this country today. According to the National Law Center on Homelessness and Poverty, in any given year, more than 3 million people in the United States are homeless—including 1.3 million children.[3] While many in this country have learned to ignore this problem—writing off the vast majority of homeless people as "bums" who are too lazy to work, or too mentally deranged to become contributing members of society—the reality of the situation is that the reasons for homelessness are numerous, and many Americans are just a paycheck or two (or a natural disaster, like Hurricane Katrina) away from homelessness themselves. Truth be told, more than 30 million Americans live at or below the poverty line, and about half of the country's home-less men and women have jobs but don't make enough to pay for housing.[4]

But, regardless of the reasons behind adult homelessness, it is the homeless children of these adults who suffer the most. They didn't ask to be homeless, they didn't decide not to eat today, and they didn't think it would be a good idea to skip out on school. Homeless children are a time bomb waiting to go off. Without the nurturing environment, healthy food, and educational opportunities that other children can count on while growing up, homeless children are on a pathway to almost certain failure—before they even get started. Many will themselves become—like their parents—disenfranchised from society, failing to learn the living skills and to develop the social networks necessary to become self-sufficient when they reach adulthood.

Studies show that, compared with their low-income peers who live in homes, homeless children experience more health problems, developmental delays, increased anxiety, depression, behavioral problems, and lower educational achievement.

It was this particular problem of homeless children that Linda Mason and Roger Brown decided to address when they and a few friends from Yale, Michael Eisenson and Jim Levitt, founded Horizons for Homeless Children, dedicated to pursuing a simple mission: to improve the lives of homeless children and their families. Estimates put the Massachusetts homeless children population at about 96,000 with half of that number under the age of five. Horizons for Homeless Children works its magic in four key ways:

1. *Playspace programs.* In its Playspace programs, Horizons for Homeless Children collaborates with residents and staff of family homeless shelters to design and build age-appropriate, kid-friendly spaces. Each Playspace is equipped with a variety of things to challenge participating

children both physically and creatively, including art supplies, building blocks, books, and more. In addition, Horizons for Homeless Children recruits, trains, places, and supervises Playspace volunteers. These volunteers—known as Playspace Activity Leaders (PALs), currently numbering more than 1,000—engage in educational play activities in more than 130 Massachusetts family shelters. Overall, more than 8,500 people have been trained to become PALs.

2. *Community Children's Centers.* Horizons for Homeless Children operates three Community Children's Centers in the Boston area to provide high-quality care to homeless children living in Boston shelters. At the heart of the Community Children's Center experiences are early education and play opportunities meant to help the 175 full-time enrolled children—age 2 months to 6 years old—learn and grow in healthy ways. An added benefit of the child care provided by the Centers is that parents are freed up to participate in a variety of on-site programs, including counseling, education, job training, and parenting workshops that can help build the competencies needed to transition to social and economic self-sufficiency. Community Children's Center staff members are given specialized training to identify developmental delays among participating children, and then to develop strategies and plans for addressing these shortcomings. The teaching curriculum focuses specifically on the developmental needs of homeless children and a low child-to-adult ratio is maintained to ensure that the children get plenty of attention from and one-on-one interaction with teachers and volunteers. In addition, a staff of Family Advocates—trained, licensed social workers—help parents obtain the services that they and their children need.

3. *Training and technical assistance.* Horizons for Homeless Children freely shares its methods and expertise with others interested in working with homeless children and their families. Over the years, the organization has developed a large body of knowledge and skills in dealing with the needs of its clients. By sharing its expertise with other organizations, Horizons for Homeless Children leverages its own efforts and amplifies their effect—helping even more homeless children and their families. Organizations and individuals who have found Horizons' skills and knowledge quite valuable

include teachers in Head Start and similar early education programs, social workers who work with homeless families in shelters, health care workers—especially in hospital emergency rooms and community health centers—who routinely treat homeless children, and homeless shelter workers themselves, who may be inadequately trained, if they are trained at all.

4. *Public policy and advocacy initiative.* Working directly with homeless children and their families is Horizons for Homeless Children's primary way of addressing the needs of their clients. The organization also utilizes a policy and advocacy initiative to directly impact legislative action and regulatory policies pertaining to the homeless. The goals of Horizons for Homeless Children is to effect policy changes that ensure homeless people have access to the services they need to be able to move to self-sufficiency by removing the legislative barriers that often get in their way.

Linda Mason and Roger Brown have been and are still involved in a variety of business pursuits. Linda is chairman of Bright Horizons Family Solutions and was the first graduate of Yale School of Management to serve on the Yale University Board of Trustees. Roger is vice chairman of Bright Horizons Family Solutions, president of the renowned Berklee College of Music in Boston, and is a trustee of Wheaton College in Massachusetts. But they remain involved in supporting the missions of the nonprofits that they founded. Both Linda and Roger serve on the board of Horizons for Homeless Children. Together, they have committed themselves to breaking the cycle of child and family homelessness.

And, based on their track record so far, they just might succeed.

Q&A WITH LINDA MASON AND ROGER BROWN, COFOUNDERS OF BRIGHT HORIZONS FOR CHILDREN (BOSTON, MASSACHUSETTS)

Giving Back: What events took place that made you to decide to give back?

Linda Mason: Roger and I had spent several years working in refugee programs overseas on the border of Cambodia and Sudan. We had been working with the most impoverished segments of the population. We came back to the States in 1986 and ended up starting a for-profit company called Bright Horizons that set up high-quality child care at the work center as a benefit program for employees. We found that we were serving dual-career couples. This was in the late 1980s, when New England was doing little for people in need— the numbers were hopeless, most notably the number of homeless families with children and single moms. This segment of the population was getting almost no services here. Children of the homeless were just falling through the cracks and getting no help at all.

Giving Back: How old were you at the time that you decided to do this?

Linda Mason: We were in our early 30s.

Giving Back: What were you doing and planning to do that gave you sufficient confidence to conclude you would give back?

Roger Brown: We had confidence because the business we had started was really exciting. It wasn't really clear if it was going to succeed. I think we just believed enough in what we were doing to hope it would succeed.

Giving Back: Were there any individuals who were a prime factor in your deciding to give back?

Linda Mason: In addition to ourselves, we had this Yale classmate, Michael Eisenson, who was in private equity who also drove this idea of serving homeless children. He was a huge force in helping launch Horizons for Homeless Children. Yale School of Management trained young people to manage in the for-profit, nonprofit, or public sectors. There is a real sense of developing leadership skills to give back to the greater good into their communities. So I think we were immersed in this sense of using our skills to create enterprise, but also to help those who were in need.

Giving Back: Did you have friends or acquaintances who discouraged you?

Linda Mason: We did not advertise that we were doing a nonprofit with our financial backers because we had just raised venture capital in 1986. We started this child care company, and then two years later while we were in operation and losing money, we started this nonprofit to give back to homeless children, and we were worried that our investors might wonder about their investment. They were always a little worried in the beginning that at some point we might decide to go back to Africa and do that kind of work. I wouldn't say we hid it from them, but we certainly didn't advertise the fact with them that we had started this nonprofit. However, I think we were wrong to do so because a few years later when our work with homeless children started to take off, our investors found out about it and they were all extremely supportive. Every single one of our venture capitalists ended up getting involved with Horizons for Homeless Children. Now, 18 years later, our business investors have given funds to our nonprofit, helping to raise $25 million in our capital campaign.

Giving Back: Why did you decide that you wanted to give back by opening Horizons for Homeless Children? You could have done so many things.

Roger Brown: We were providing child care to all the working parents, and we could see how good it was for their children and our own children. So we thought, "Isn't it a shame that the poorest people, the homeless, nowhere to go, don't have access to facilities for their children, and with all this deprivation and trouble with being homeless already, wouldn't it be great if they had a child care center they could go to?" Then it dawned on us that the only way the mothers who were homeless were going to get job training and be able to get back on track and get a house again was to get a job. The only way they could do that if they had young children was to have child care, which could be strategically a very powerful inter-vention to prevent them from missing out on those first five years of development. It could also allow the parents to have enough cushion in their lives to get back on track.

Giving Back: What is the most significant contribution you have made with your leadership skills?

Roger Brown: I think the most significant thing we did was that we didn't try to run or micromanage the organization. We had other things to do. We built a very strong board, we hired a very strong executive director whom we were extremely supportive of, and basically allowed the organization to pursue it own path and its own destiny. I think we had a good idea, we got the thing pointed in the right direction, we got enough resources in place to figure out what to do and hired some people to do it, and recruited a good board to support it. And we also incubated it in a sense. We allowed it to piggyback on the payroll, accounting, office space, and architecture of Bright Horizons. It's now totally independent of all that. It was in the early days, when it really had very few resources, that we supported it that way.

Giving Back: What is the most significant contribution you made with your financial resources? Was it to get started?

Roger Brown: I think we have recently made what for us is a very large financial gift. It is a small part of the whole. In the beginning we were the whole thing. We found a foundation to give us a start-up grant. We put in some of our own money, and we helped to get other people to support it. I think that a dollar when you are starting something is bigger than a dollar when you have an $8 or $9 million budget.

Giving Back: What changes, if any, would you make today in your initial approach?

Linda Mason: The hard part about that question is when you talk to entrepreneurs, they don't look back with a lot or regrets or wish they had done something else. It's been such a successful organization.

Roger Brown: I think there was some early wandering around looking for exactly what to do. It feels like that is an essential part of making sure you are doing the right thing and experimenting with a few things. Even though it wasn't a linear path, I think there was a lot of growth and learning that came out of it.

Giving Back: How have you been able to interest people in working for a nonprofit organization?

Linda Mason: Let me start with the Board. We have an extremely strong Board; one of the strongest in greater Boston. I think one thing we did early on that has been very successful is attracting volunteer Board members to work on behalf of the organization. We try to put in young, private equity folks. These are people in their 30s that are working for venture capital firms, private equity firms, and since they are in their 30s, most of them are typically married with a couple of young children. So they and their spouses relate to this issue of homeless children. By engaging them early on, they feel they have a personal connection they can relate to because of their young children. Second, they are early enough in their career that for most of them they have not yet adopted a major philanthropy to support, so we became their philanthropy to support, and as their careers have taken off, their giving potential has taken off, so it's created a very strong core of supporters, and we appeal to the whole family. We have found ways for the families to be involved, whether it's volunteering at the center, doing toy drives, or fund-raising drives. So I think that's on the board side.

Roger Brown: The beauty of a good nonprofit's doing important work is that it will attract people in and of itself. The Horizons for Homeless Children is now, we think, the largest volunteer organization in the whole state of Massachusetts—we have a thousand volunteers. As long as there is integrity and enough strength to make it—and people have an opportunity to solve problems and be with people who have worked there—they will stay engaged. I do think having a well-defined mission that is narrowly focused so people can get their arms around it, and it clearly is serving an important cause, coupled with integrity, means more people believe that there will be viability.

Linda Mason: We think it's a very well-run organization. We have had the same executive director for 15 years, and she has a very good sense of sound fiscal management. One of the biggest problems in nonprofits is that ability. I do think talented people see this as an organization that operates with a very supportive board, so it feels like they are not taking as much of a risk—that it's an organization that is here to stay.

Giving Back: Do any of the volunteers come from business organizations?

Roger Brown: A lot of businesses actually come to our community service project, where they will paint a center or help set one up. There are a myriad of volunteer opportunities for businesspeople. Most of the people who are volunteers are professionals by day who want to do something constructive. In the beginning that was just a small piece of what we did. But, again, we found that people really loved the idea of spending some time with young children, particularly homeless children and children who have been through such trauma as young kids. We now have over 100 play spaces in homeless shelters where homeless kids can go and read and play and have blocks and puzzles and that sort of thing. Volunteers work there two hours a week, every week, to staff those play spaces. It is evident there is a strong demand for it, and we have a really good volunteer training program. It just took off. It's a huge part of the program. Because more than just giving a child important learning tools for play, a caring person is there with them. Another benefit is that a lot of those volunteers, themselves, are financially supportive of the organization.

Giving Back: What corporate executive do you admire most for their contributions, personal and philanthropic?

Roger Brown: There's no one more philanthropic than Bill Gates in our generation.

Linda Mason: And, I think, closer to home, our very first investor, Josh Berkenstein, who is the managing director of Bain Capital. He's someone we admire enormously for his philanthropic and personal commitment, in addition to being an outstanding professional. Josh and Michael Eisenson have both been critical to the success of Horizons for Homeless Children as well as other nonprofits.

Roger Brown: I know someone whom we both really admire. It is Jim Rouse. He started a company that did redevelopment of cities; he redeveloped Faneuil Hall and the South Street Seaport, and outside of Baltimore he created the city of Columbia, Maryland. Then he decided to retire from business and focus all his energies on housing and started this organization called the Enterprise Foundation. He's a real inspiration. In thinking back on it, he tried to recruit us right about the time we were starting Bright Horizons; and we didn't join him, but I think his ability to combine business and philanthropy was a real inspiration to us. He was a very progressive thinker and visionary. He wouldn't let anything get in his way.

Giving Back: What societal needs are you most concerned about?

Roger Brown: I'm most concerned about poverty and racism in this country. And, of course, they are interwoven. Internationally, I think we worry about wars and conflicts and where you have people wielding power over the helpless and they have no recourse.

The biggest creator of world poverty is civil wars and internal conflicts within countries and across borders.

Linda Mason: I worry increasingly about climate change and its disproportionate impact on the poorest countries and the poorest people in the world. I just went to a conference on climate change yesterday at the Lincoln Institute of Land Policy, run by Jim Levitt, that was fantastic.

Giving Back: What is your personal philosophy that energizes and motivates you?

Roger Brown: I like to create things that didn't exist before. I love the idea of looking at an organization and thinking that this didn't exist at all, and we and a few other friends dreamed it up, thought of a name to call it, got some people involved, focused on a mission in due time, and it develops.

Linda Mason: One thing that has always been very important to me is this whole issue of touching lives one by one. Having spent years working in crisis environments in the developing world, it could easily feel overwhelming. But then when you start getting involved, you realize you are helping that one life in front of you, and then the next life, and the next life. You may not be able to solve all the problems, but you can solve some problems in front of you.

Notes

1. Mark Small, "Roger Brown: Mission Driven," *Berklee Today,* (Fall 2004).
2. http://eclips.cornell.edu/interviewLecture.do?id=8&clipID=1543&tab=TabClipPage.
3. www.nlchp.org/hapia.cfm (accessed August 26, 2007).
4. www.nlchp.org/hapia_causes.cfm (accessed August 26, 2007).

CHAPTER 6

Fried Chicken, Foster Children, and Chick-fil-A

A good name is rather to be chosen than great riches, and loving favour rather than silver and gold.

—PROVERBS 22:1

Ask S. Truett Cathy to autograph one of his books for you (he's written a number of them, including *The Generosity Factor* [Zondervan, 2002] with business guru Ken Blanchard, *Eat Mor Chikin: Inspire More People* [Looking Glass Books, 2002], and *It's Better to Build Boys than Mend Men* [Looking Glass Books, 2004]), and chances are that he will include the following inscription after his signature: Proverbs 22:1. The meaning of this biblical passage (quoted above) is simple, yet profound: even though money is valuable, other things—specifically, integrity, honor, and gaining the trust of others—are even more valuable. Truett Cathy—founder and chairman of the fast-growing, privately held Chick-fil-A fast-food restaurant chain—has taken this passage to heart, living a life that is both an inspiring success story and a living demonstration of how deep commitment to giving back to his community can make a very real difference in the lives of thousands of people.

By every measure, Truett Cathy is a success. Today, the company he founded operates more than 1,300 restaurants in 37 states and Washington, D.C., and it brings in sales of more than $2 billion a year—making it the second largest quick-service chicken restaurant chain in the nation. But every story of great business success starts somewhere, and for Truett Cathy—who invented the boneless breast of chicken sandwich (the "Chick-fil-A") in the early 1960s—this story started in 1946, when Truett and his brother Ben opened the Dwarf Grill in Hapeville, Georgia, a suburb of Atlanta. The Grill—open for business 24 hours a day—was aptly named (and subsequently renamed the Dwarf House), with only four tables in the small dining room and 10 stools along the service counter for customers to sit. The first day's sales? $58.20. Truett lived in a room next door to the Dwarf House, and when things got busy—day or night—he would make the short walk to the restaurant to help out. Unfortunately, Ben died in a private airplane accident a few years after starting the restaurant, but Truett pressed on, steadily growing the business. In 1951, Truett opened a second Dwarf House, this one in Forest Park, another suburb of Atlanta.

While the business was doing all right, it wasn't until 1967 when things would begin to take a dramatic turn upwards. It was in this year that Truett opened the first Chick-fil-A fast-food restaurant—not only pioneering the marketing of the fast-serve chicken breast sandwich, but also pioneering a new location for restaurants of any sort: the shopping mall (specifically, the Greenbrier Mall in Atlanta, Georgia). From these humble beginnings, the Chick-fil-A restaurant chain grew—and grew and grew. This despite a corporate policy that is unique in the fast-food industry: Every Chick-fil-A restaurant is closed on Sunday. Why? Because the deeply religious Cathy firmly believes that it is important for employees to have the opportunity to relax and recharge—and attend church—if they so desire on Sunday. Says Truett: "Maybe I'm losing 20% on sales, because Sunday is a big day. But it's the policy we established back in 1946, and we dare not vary from that. We've been profitable. I think it's probably the best business decision I've made, because that's what attracted employees who appreciated having Sunday off."[1]

Indeed, the loyalty that employees feel for Chick-fil-A and for Truett Cathy is extraordinary. In an industry where employee turnover rates of 100% or more (sometimes *much* more) are the norm and not the exception, Chick-fil-A stands heads and shoulders above its peers with an employee turnover rate of only about 4%. Some of the company's veteran employees have been with Chick-fil-A for more than 30 years. Part of the reason is that they are treated with a level of respect that few other quick-service restaurants can equal. But another reason is surely the loyalty that the company itself shows its employees.

In 1973—just six years after the first Chick-fil-A restaurant opened—Truett Cathy inaugurated the Team Member Scholarship Program (replaced by the Leadership Scholarship program in 1996), providing eligible employees with $1,000 college scholarships. In 1997, the company awarded the first S. Truett Cathy Scholar Awards to the year's top 25 Leadership Scholarship recipients. These awards provided the winners with an additional $1,000 toward their education. More than $23 million in scholarships have been distributed to more than 20,000 employees since 1973 as a result of these programs. In 2007 alone, the company will grant more than $1.3 million in scholarships to Chick-fil-A employees through the Leadership Scholarship program and S. Truett Cathy Scholar Awards.

In 1975, the company began the Symbol of Success program to recognize Chick-fil-A Operators (franchisees/owners) who meet or exceed their annual sales goals. This program awarded the free use of a Ford automobile to the lucky Operators for an entire year. In 1983, a record 46 cars were provided through the Symbol of Success program, and in 2006, the number of vehicles rocketed to 164. In 2002, Chick-fil-A was awarded the Employer of Choice Award by the National Restaurant Association, and the chain was voted Best Drive-Thru in America by *QSR* magazine.

However, throughout this long period of growth and business success, Truett Cathy never forgot about the importance of giving back to the larger community outside of his business. He began by teaching Sunday school classes to 11-year-old boys—instilling within them the kind of values that some were not receiving at home. Says Cathy, "But all children need strong adult role models, and many of them, even back then, weren't seeing them at home. I enjoyed treating the boys to dinner at the Dwarf House one night during the week. It was a good time for us to get to know each other between Sundays."[2] When a customer ended up in the hospital, Truett and his brother Ben would send food to their house, to help out their family. And when a customer died, they would also send food to the family.

In 1984, Truett created the WinShape Foundation to help build character in the lives of young people—in the words of the Foundation, to "shape winners." The first initiative for the Foundation was the WinShape College

Program. Partnering with Rome, Georgia's Berry College, the Foundation provides scholarships in the total amount of $32,000 for up to four years of schooling. The college prides itself on furthering its students' intellectual, moral, and spiritual growth by way of lessons that are gained from worth-while work done well—challenging students to devote their learning to community and civic betterment. And, while applicants for the scholar-ships to Berry College are not required to have experience working for Chick-fil-A, priority is given to Chick-fil-A veterans. Approximately 120 students participate in the WinShape Foundation scholarship program each year, living on campus in two special WinShape dormitories.

But not only did Truett Cathy's partnership with Berry College create the scholarship program, it helped to save Berry itself. When Truett first met with Dr. Gloria Shatto, Berry's president, the school's board of trustees had decided to close the Mountain Campus boarding school which served children in the fifth through twelfth grades at Berry. Why? Because the boarding school was losing $2 million a year. After much thought and discussion with his wife Jeannette, Truett came up with a vision for the future of the Mountain Campus of Berry College—a vision that included housing for Berry students who would receive scholarships from Chick-fil-A, a foster home for promising children who through no fault of their own had fallen on hard times, and a summer camp for chil-dren. Dr. Shatto readily agreed with and supported Truett's ideas.

Chick-fil-A's executive committee, however, was not as excited about Truett's vision, instead siding with the Berry board of trustees idea of closing down the campus and stemming the flow of financial red ink. The members of the executive committee thought that taking on a project of this magnitude would be a mistake, and they were candid with Truett in this assessment. However, Truett was not to be dissuaded from achieving his vision, and he forged on. Soon, the WinShape College Program was open for business, providing 68 students with $10,000 scholarships in 1984, its first year of operations.

The WinShape Foundation—under Truett Cathy's guidance—has expanded from this original initiative into a variety of different programs. These programs include:

- *WinShape Camps.* Founded in 1985 by Truett Cathy, WinShape Camps are specifically designed to provide young people with a

12-day, residential summer recreational experience for 1,800 boys and girls designed to challenge campers, sharpen their character, and deepen their faith and relationships. Camps offer a variety of activities, including sports, wall climbing, arts and crafts, rope and adventure challenge courses, and much more. The Camps have recently branched out with the Great Family Weekend Adventure, which invites entire families to enjoy the camp experience.

- *WinShape Homes.* Founded in 1987 by Truett Cathy, WinShape Homes provides a loving, nurturing home to foster children "who are victims of circumstance and need a stable, secure family environment in which to grow and mature." There are currently 12 WinShape Homes—11 in the Southern United States, and one in Brazil. Homes are designed to accommodate up to 12 children and employ full-time house parents. Boys and girls are eligible to participate, without regard to their race, culture, or religion, and WinShape Homes provides large sibling groups with the unique opportunity to live together in the same home. Homes encourage the children's participation in extracurricular activities and provide services to meet the children's physical, spiritual, and emotional needs.
- *WinShape Wilderness.* Founded in 1991, the goal of WinShape Wilderness is to lead thousands of people into adventure-learning experiences, including rope courses and outdoor team-building programs. Working with participants from church leadership and mission teams to youth, college students, corporate training, and marriage groups, WinShape Wilderness creates experiences customized to meet the needs of participating teams, as well as signature courses in community building and leadership development.
- *WinShape Retreat.* Located within a wildlife refuge at the Mountain Campus of Berry College near Rome, Georgia, WinShape Retreat offers groups and individuals alike the opportunity to unplug from their hectic day-to-day lives to relax and reflect. There are no TVs, telephones, or Internet connections in WinShape Retreat's 62 rooms—just 300 acres of beautiful grounds ready for hiking, exploring, and wildlife watching. Regular activities include hayrides, bonfires, horseback riding, and even a rope course for group team-building exercises.

- *WinShape Marriage.* This program is designed to help couples build healthy marriages by establishing healthy priorities, managing home and business, increasing intimacy, and rekindling passion in marriage. Conducted within a wildlife refuge at the Mountain Campus of Berry College near Rome, Georgia, WinShape Marriage offers moderately priced courses with such names as Romantic Adventure, Follow Your Heart, Prepare to Last, and Couples Intensive. There is even a Caribbean Sailing Adventure for particularly adventurous couples.

- *WinShape International.* WinShape International—the most recent program of the WinShape Foundation—is devoted to helping young adults become Christian leaders within their own cultures. The organization's mission is to mobilize leaders (primarily Chick-fil-A corporate staff, owners/operators, and their team leaders) to transform young people and communities around the world. WinShape International currently has active projects in South Africa, India, Sudan, and Zambia.

CASESTUDY

7 REMINDERS FOR BUILDING CHILDREN*
BY S. TRUETT CATHY, FOUNDER
AND CHAIRMAN OF CHICK-FIL-A

1. Every child I know who overcame long odds and grew into a responsible adult can point to an adult who stepped into his or her life as a friend, mentor, and guide.
2. Don't be too concerned that your children don't listen to you. But be very concerned that they see everything you do.
3. Be so consistent in your discipline that you're boring.
4. Stop arguing in front of your children.
5. You may think children have outgrown the desire to be rocked to sleep at night. They haven't.

---

*Excerpted from Cathy's 2004 book: *It's Better to Build Boys Than Mend Men*, Looking Glass Books.

6. Children will never believe in the covenant of marriage unless they see you living it with their own eyes.
7. How do you know if a child needs encouragement? If he or she is breathing.

S. Truett Cathy was born to poverty in 1921. However, through much hard work and perseverance, Truett built a business that today brings in more than $2 billion a year. But rather than seeking riches for himself, Truett has devoted his life to serving others—including his family, his customers, his employees, the 150 foster children who call him "Grandpa," and the larger community in which he lives. He still teaches Sunday school at First Baptist Church in Jonesboro, Georgia (although he has moved from teaching 11-year-olds to teaching 13-year olds)— more than 50 years after teaching his first class—and he still believes that the more he gives, the more he gets back. Says Cathy, "Nearly every moment of every day we have the opportunity to give something to someone else—our time, our love, our resources. I have always found more joy in giving when I did not expect anything in return."

Q&A WITH S. TRUETT CATHY, FOUNDER OF CHICK-FIL-A (ATLANTA, GEORGIA)

Giving Back: What events took place that helped you decide you wanted to give back?

Truett Cathy: I was born in poverty. My mother was the breadwinner, and it was at an early age that she opened a boarding house. We furnished a bed in a room and charged a dollar a day—$7 a week— for room and board. And I learned how to shuck corn and shell peas and wash dishes and set the table. I belong to the First Baptist Church of Jonesboro, Georgia. My pastor asked, "What did Jesus say that few people believe?" The answer was simply that it is better to give than to receive. There are very few people who have found this out. It seems to me like the more I give, the more I have. I think a lot of people have missed the joy of giving. We are all created in the image of the Lord, and everything He created was for the purpose of giving. The trees I'm looking at from my office, the ground, the stars, and the moon and human beings—we are all created for the purpose of giving. We are living in a greater world nowadays, asking, "What will somebody do for me?" We have our priorities all mixed up. If we are looking to give, I think the blessings will be restored upon a person. There is a great satisfaction in giving, especially when you don't expect to get anything in return. This is a natural thing—God's creation—with the purpose of giving.

Giving Back: How old were you when you came to the conclusion that you wanted to give back?

Truett Cathy: Throughout my business life. I've been in business for over 61 years—in 2006, I celebrated my 60th year in the restaurant business at the same location. I don't know of anybody who has been in business anyplace for that length of time. I've been in the restaurant business serving the physical and emotional needs of people, and oftentimes their spiritual needs. I feel like it's a high calling to have that position of furnishing the essentials of life, and not just food, itself. Going back to the biblical principle, I want to believe the Bible is a road map, a blueprint of my life. I have not only read it, but practiced it. I have lived in poverty—I had to work for what I have—and I always believed that the harder you work, the more successful you become. I started out at eight years old buying Cokes, six for a quarter, and selling them for a nickel apiece and recognizing a 5-cent profit. A full case of Coca-Cola was 24 Cokes for 80 cents; you sell 24 Cokes for 5 cents apiece, and you made yourself 40 cents. To me, that was big business. From there, I sold magazines, and I got a paper route. I would tell my people if they would get their paper from me, I would put it by the screen door or put it up on the porch. I would be there rain or shine. I was a pretty good salesman in that period of time. Then I had a gift for buying something wholesale and selling it retail.

Giving Back: What individuals were key to your deciding to give back?

Truett Cathy: The most positive were my mom, my wife, and the Sunday school teacher I had when I was a teenager. He was very kind to me and he was a role model for me. He helped me with my papers on Sunday morning. My dad was not the kind of father that I could go to when I had a problem. He was there, and that's about the only contact I had with him. We're still a private company, and I intend to stay that way. We give out a lot of things we couldn't do if we were a pubic company. We have a scholarship program for our part-time team members, where we give them $1,000 scholarships if they work for us for two years. Our average work schedule is 20 hours a week. We've devoted millions of dollars toward that, and the other scholarship programs we have. We have a boy's camp and a girl's camp, and I have 12 foster homes where we try to identify those kids who do not have any serious behavior problems, just victims of circumstances. I agree that it seems like the more you give, the more you have. I have all the things I ever wanted material-wise, as well as awards from my family and grandchildren, and the foster kids that I have had. I have supported foster homes for 20 years. Some of them have been a total disappointment, and others have been very rewarding.

Giving Back: In your lifetime, were there any people who tried to discourage you from giving back?

Truett Cathy: I don't think anybody has discouraged me from giving.

Giving Back: What's the most significant contribution you have made with your leadership skills?

Truett Cathy: The most significant thing, I think, would be the example I have tried to set for other people, even with our family, that I tried to not dictate, but demonstrate what I'm trying to say and what I'm trying to do. I have a moral and corporate compass to glorify God by being a faithful steward. That means to give back a portion of God's blessings to others, and to help the people we come in contact with.

Giving Back: How do you interest people in working for a nonprofit organization as a volunteer?

Truett Cathy: I'm talking about Boy Scouts, and things of this sort that I'm involved in—social services, hospice care, the hospital and prevention of AIDS. I have been involved in a lot of programs such as that, but not recently. I've been a person who gets involved with kids, who coaches football and baseball games. I have a book out, *It's Better to Build Boys than Mend Men.* I have been teaching 13-year-old boys in Sunday school for 51 years. At least from the experience I have had some influence on young people. They must suffer the consequences for their bad decisions. You can't blame your parents or lack of parents.

Giving Back: In these various philanthropic organizations with which you are involved, are you involved personally, or do you also involve your company?

Truett Cathy: I was and am involved personally. I tell the kids that they don't have to listen to others, but it could be worthwhile. I play their own grandpa for them. I tell them they don't have to call me their grandpa, but I'm personally involved with them. I can't personally spend time with them like I used to. I used to have them in my own home, but now I can't take them on trips with me, and lots of other things. I do still give them my time.

Giving Back: What corporate executives do you admire most for the contributions they have made to their communities?

Truett Cathy: I like J.B. Fuqua—he has been very generous. He once told me, "Truett, it seems like the more money I give, the more I have." He has given away more than $150 million for various causes. He doesn't seem to get involved in it, but he's done a lot of good things. He was also a great benefactor.

Notes

1. Tom Neven, "A Doer of the Word,"*Focus on the Family,* September 2000.
2. S. Truett Cathy, *Eat Mor Chikin: Inspire More People*. Looking Glass Books, 2002. p. 40.

CHAPTER 7

Mixing Principles and Profits at Stonyfield Farm

Every time I've done the right thing for the environment, I've made a profit.

—YVON CHOUINARD

Just one look at Stonyfield Farm's logo tells you almost everything you need to know about where the company's heart—and its mission—lies: "Stonyfield Farm—For a Healthy Planet." While the company's tagline might seem conveniently trendy nowadays—after all, who isn't for a healthy planet?—the truth is that Stonyfield Farm (which today is the world's leading producer of organic yogurt) was a pioneer in the organic food industry, creating markets and pushing its healthy food/sustainable agriculture agenda years before most other food producers. And while other companies may talk a lot about making the world a better place—and make a generous contribution or two to worthy organizations such as the Nature Conservancy or Susan G. Komen for the Cure along the way—Stonyfield Farm does far more than just contribute money to the causes in which it believes. It designs, creates, and executes a dizzying variety of initiatives to help create a healthy planet, and it has teamed with numerous like-minded organizations to further its own mission.

And it makes money—lots of money.

Stonyfield Farm—headquartered in Londonderry, New Hampshire—has deep roots in the organic food movement of the late 1960s and early 1970s. In fact, its original incarnation was as the Rural Education Center, a small organic farming school that needed a way to earn money to further its social mission—a mission that current Stonyfield chairman, president, and "CE-Yo" Gary Hirshberg and the company's employees and suppliers are committed to even today. Although Samuel and Louise Kaymen established the Rural Education Center in 1979—and it was Samuel who perfected the yogurt recipe that became the foundation of Stonyfield Farm Yogurt—it was Gary Hirshberg who brought business smarts to the table when he was tapped to join the Center's board in 1982. Gary's job was to help develop and implement a business strategy for the Center and to generate financial support.

And what was the strategy that Gary ultimately recommended? To expand the farm and turn its small-scale yogurt production into a moneymaking operation.

With Gary's vision for the future and a $35,000 loan from the Institute for Community Economics, Stonyfield Farm was born in 1983. Soon after, the company—using the milk produced from its seven Jersey cows—produced its very first batch of yogurt. By the end of the year, production steadily climbed to 150 cases a week. But, like any small business start-up, Stonyfield went through its share of ups and downs—and more than a few near-death experiences.

There were the times, for example, when the power to the barn went out and Gary, Louise, Samuel, and various family members would have to milk the cows themselves—by hand. Or when every winter—like clockwork—pipes would freeze, pumps would break down, and the trucks used to transport Stonyfield's yogurt to market would get stuck on the winding dirt road leading to the farm. Or when—in 1987—Stonyfield's copacker went bankrupt, almost dragging Stonyfield along with it when the bank shut down production and seized the company's yogurt-production equipment. Or even when, after moving to a new plant in 1989, the initial batches of yogurt refused to thicken—resulting in a liquid version of the product that was unusable.

Fortunately, these problems were solved, and the company thrived. Stonyfield Farm has experienced a compounded annual growth rate of 27.4% for more than 18 years by consistently producing a quality product and using innovative marketing techniques that blend the company's social, environmental, and financial missions. Today, the company's annual revenues stand at more than $300 million, and Stonyfield is the leading producer of organic yogurt in the world. At Stonyfield, principles and profits are mixed to create an organization like few others. In an article in *Leader to Leader* magazine, Gary Hirshberg put his company's unique approach in perspective: "At Stonyfield Farm . . . our values and social mission are central to everything we do, and they are embedded deeply in our organizational DNA. We are in business, for sure, to make a profit, but we are in business to do far more than simply achieve a positive financial goal. We are in business to change the world."[1]

And, in its own way and on its own schedule, one step at a time, that is exactly what Stonyfield Farm is doing. For while Stonyfield is indeed in business to make a profit and to return value to its investors, the company's mission statement clearly indicates where its priorities lie.

CASESTUDY	THE STONYFIELD FARM MISSION

- To provide the very highest-quality, best-tasting, all-natural, and certified organic products.
- To educate consumers and producers about the value of protecting the environment, and of supporting family farmers and sustainable farming methods.
- To serve as a model that environmentally and socially responsible businesses can also be profitable.
- To provide a healthful, productive, and enjoyable workplace for all employees, with opportunities to gain new skills and advance personal career goals.
- To recognize our obligations to stockholders and lenders by providing an excellent return on their investment.

To support its vision of a healthy planet, and to make progress in achieving its mission, Stonyfield takes a four-pronged approach:

1. Using the best environmental practices we can find.
2. Supporting family farms and organic agriculture.
3. Giving profits to the earth.
4. Learning what we can do.

Stonyfield's Profits to the Planet program has become an extremely effective way for the company to give back, while supporting organizations that believe in its social mission. Under this program, Stonyfield has committed to giving away 10% of its profits to organizations and projects that work to protect and restore the earth. In 2006, for example, this commitment amounted to more than $1 million in grants to nonprofit and educational organizations nationwide to support environmental and organic programs. Some of the recipients included:

- *American Farmland Trust,* an organization that works to protect the more than 1 million acres of American farmland currently in danger of being developed and taken out of agricultural use.
- *Clean Air—Cool Planet,* which advises businesses on energy efficiency, clean energy, and climate-friendly transportation options.
- *Healthy Food, Healthy Communities,* an organization that partnered with Hampshire College in Massachusetts to provide fresh fruit and vegetables to low-income families.
- *Organic Farming Research Institute,* which helped initiate 11 new organic farming research and education projects.
- *World Media Foundation—Living on Earth,* which produces a weekly environmental news and information program broadcast on 302 National Public Radio stations across the country.

Stonyfield has long been in the vanguard of American companies that are doing something about climate change and global warming, reducing its own impact on the planet. To accomplish this goal, Stonyfield has pursued a five-part approach:

1. *Improving efficiency to reduce global warming gases.* Over the past 10 years, Stonyfield Farm has saved more than 46 million kilowatt hours (equating to more than $1.7 million) of energy by designing and implementing more efficient methods of yogurt production.
2. *Incorporating renewables.* In 2005, Stonyfield built the largest solar energy installation in New Hampshire—a 50-kilowatt solar photovoltaic array—at its Londonderry yogurt plant.
3. *Offsetting the global warming emissions from our facility energy use.* Despite its efforts, Stonyfield still produces greenhouse gases. The company was the first U.S. manufacturer to offset 100% of its CO_2 emissions. Over the past ten years, the company has offset

more than 40,000 metric tons of global warming gases, which is the equivalent of taking more than 7,000 cars off the road for an entire year.

4. *Reducing packaging and solid waste.* By reducing and recycling its waste, Stonyfield Farm helps reduce the amount of petroleum required for their manufacture, saving energy and lowering emissions. Just switching from a plastic to an aluminum lid for its yogurt cups eliminated a requirement for more than 270 tons of plastic each year—saving enough energy to power more than 180 American households for one year.

5. *Supporting organic farming.* Each year, the Stonyfield buys millions of pounds of organic ingredients to manufacture its products, including primarily the milk used in its yogurt, ice cream, and smoothies.

Speaking of organics, Stonyfield has never forgotten that it started its life as an organic farming educational center. As of October 2007, all of Stonyfield Farm's products are certified organic, that is, grown without the use of pesticides and petroleum-based fertilizers. The company has taken very strong positions against the use of genetically modified organisms (GMOs), was an early leader in the campaign against the widespread use of recombinant bovine growth hormone (rBGH), which is used by dairy farms to artificially increase milk production in cows, and has lobbied for more humane treatment of farm animals, arguing that cows should be well-fed, well-housed, protected from extreme weather conditions, and have access to pastureland during the summer months.

To help reduce the amount of plastic waste entering landfills, Stonyfield has partnered with Waltham, Massachusetts–based Recycline to recycle its used yogurt cups into the production of toothbrushes and razors. The handles of these Recycline products currently consist of between 25 to 65% recycled Stonyfield yogurt cup plastic. When these toothbrushes and razors have reached the end of their useful lives, they can be sent back to Recycline and exchanged for new ones—perpetuating the process.

By every measure—business and social responsibility—Stonyfield Farm has succeeded. Indeed, because of its stellar growth record—and because of the niche it had carved out of the organic foods market—Stonyfield was approached by Groupe Danone, the world's largest producer of fresh dairy products, as an acquisition target. After two years of on-again, off-again negotiations, in 2001 Stonyfield entered into a partnership with

Groupe Danone in exchange for a 40% stake in Stonyfield. This investment was eventually increased to today's figure of 85%, with the remainder owned by Stonyfield employees.

The arrangement that Stonyfield negotiated with Groupe Danone gives the company unprecedented control over operations. Hirshberg remains in full operational control of the company while taking advantage of Groupe Danone's massive purchasing power, its economies of scale, and its extensive, worldwide distribution network.

And that's just the business side of things. On the social responsibility front, Stonyfield Farm's short history is full of accomplishments. During a 20-year period beginning in April 1983, Stonyfield:

- Recycled more than 10 million pounds of material.
- Donated more than $3 million to activities that protect and restore the earth through its Profits for the Planet program.
- Produced more than 135 unique yogurt container lids with environmental and educational messages to inform consumers and urge them to take action.
- Used over 150 million pounds of organic ingredients in the production of its yogurt and other products.
- Donated more than 4 million servings of yogurt to community events and food banks.
- Gave more than 5 million pounds of yogurt leftovers (from quality control testing and such) to farmers for feed for hogs.
- Saved more than $1 million by reducing the energy required to produce yogurt.
- Redesigned its yogurt cups to require less plastic, preventing the production and disposal of more than 700 tons of the material.

The company has racked up an enviable list of firsts, including becoming the nation's first dairy producer to pay farmers not to treat cows with the synthetic bovine growth hormone rBGH, the first American manufacturer to offset 100% of its CO_2 emissions from its facility energy use, the first for-profit corporation to register its greenhouse gas emissions with the state of New Hampshire's voluntary registry, and much more. Its efforts on behalf of the environment have won many awards, including recognition from the Environmental Protection Agency, the National Wildlife Federation, and the Department of Energy.

Many of these initiatives are a direct result of Gary Hirshberg's personal mission in life: to find ways to merge commerce and create a healthier planet. Says Gary:

> My personal mission in life was exploring if it was possible to create commerce that has a positive impact on the earth instead of a negative one. I recognized that business was a large part of the problem; that is, the fact that we were heating up the planet was the direct result of commercial activity. And so the question was this: Could we create a commercial solution or commercial model that actually rewarded the lessening of climate footprint? If we're serious about all these things—if we're serious about reducing our climate footprint, serious about saving farmers, if we're serious about taking toxins out of the ecosystem, then we can't be satisfied to just be a little club of insiders. We have to get others involved. Should we all reduce our consumption? Absolutely. Should we all live in teepees and eat within a quarter-mile of our homes? That's not going to happen. We've discovered the banana in the Northern Hemisphere, and we're not going back to not having bananas. My point is not that we should all reduce our footprint. My point is that if you're going to be consuming, consume consciously, and using your purchasing activity can make incredible change.

Perhaps as the most telling stamp of approval, Stonyfield Farm has become an important place for politicians—and political office-seekers—to see and be seen. In April 2007, Democratic presidential candidates Governor Bill Richardson of New Mexico and former Senator John Edwards of North Carolina both stopped by Stonyfield Farm to meet employees and tour the yogurt production facilities. President Bill Clinton, Vice President Al Gore, Vermont Governor Howard Dean, former Virginia Governor Mark Warner, and many others have all spent time at Stonyfield.

As the example of Gary Hirshberg and Stonyfield Farm shows, by directing the resources of your company to support a very specific set of values, you have the potential to significantly impact the world around you. And when your employees support the company's mission and values, then you've got the potential for an even greater impact. According to Hirshberg:

> What has happened in these past 25 years is that the hypotheses we worked with in building this company have become proven. We've

shown this is a way to keep money in local circulation to save farmers and get healthier food to people—creating win-win-win-win situations. So now where I have shifted my focus in the past couple of years is how to bring it to a much greater scale. Even though we can celebrate the fact that organics is now a $17.5 billion industry, it's still only 2.5% of total foods sold. And if we're serious about taking toxins out of the biosphere, and if we're serious about climate change, then we've got to work on a much larger scale.

But Hirshberg isn't one to look backward and rest on the laurels of his company's success—he is always looking forward, alert to new challenges and opportunities. Says Gary:

While climate change remains the number one issue, removing or eliminating toxins is right behind it. The interesting thing about climate change is that by addressing it, we can also address other problems. Another major concern is the current terrorism scenario that we find ourselves embroiled in globally. We're involved in a religious and class war and, ironically, what we've done is fund the protagonists by buying their oil. We have empowered a medieval kind of battle that most of us had thought we had evolved through, but we obviously were wrong. So I think that climate change is not just about climate. Climate change is also about national security, environmental security, and economic security. And it's also about creating a healthier planet.

Q&A with Gary Hirshberg, President and CEO of Stonyfield Farm (Londonderry, New Hampshire)

Giving Back: What societal needs were you most concerned about in Stonyfield's early days, and what did you do to respond to them?

Gary Hirshberg: I think the main focus for us was the contamination of our diets—especially children's diets—with a variety of things that really shouldn't be in food. We were trying to raise awareness that we are what we eat, but related to that was also the coincidental concern that we felt that family farmers needed to be recognized and supported in our society. We saw them as an endangered species and felt that consumers needed to be reminded that when they purchase food—whether they're conscious of their purchases or not—that there's a farmer somewhere back there who actually produced it. We thought that they should shift their purchases to try, where possible, to keep family farmers healthy. In the end, we kept coming back to the first concern: that there's no way for people to get healthy food, we felt, if they aren't involved in the growing of it. It was a combination of what I would call a nutritional and health mission, and kind of a social community issue. But keep in mind that when we began, we were a very local, small company. The problem of the decline of family farmers—which is ubiquitous—was especially notable here in New England where farmers were in extremely rapid decline in numbers. In fact, the number of all full-time farmers has still declined. The happy thing I can report today, 25 years later, is that the number of organic farmers has rapidly grown and the number of dairy farmers who converted over to organic has rapidly grown and, therefore, the number of organic family farmers is actually much higher than when we started all this.

Giving Back: Did you encounter resistance to your ideas?

Gary Hirshberg: Yes. It started with the old belief that supermarkets are not a place where healthy food is sold. Instead, supermarkets are places where people are going to beat up food producers and make your product cheap and reduce you to some level of mediocrity. Within the community of healthy food producers, there was fear of the business world—some of which we validated because we were pretty naïve going into it. On the one hand, everything was extremely countercultural in the mass culture sense of the word but, on the other hand, we were counterculture to the counterculture.

Giving Back: Were there role models for you along the way?

Gary Hirshberg: Oh, sure. First of all, we were inspired by Ben and Jerry's. They were seven years ahead of us. They weren't, of course, models for doing healthy food—quite the opposite. But, certainly, their idea of breaking the normal rules of business inspired us. I really need to pay deference to Ben and Jerry because they were showing not only me that it was possible, but they were also showing retailers and others. Tom and Kate Chappell [cofounders of Tom's of Maine] were inspirations. Anthony Harnett at Bread and Circus. Paul Hawken had a little-known life before he became a famous author.

He ran something called Erewhon Trading Company in Cambridge, Massachusetts, which was one of the first natural food stores. These were folks who were bringing their values to commerce. And there were people who inspired me more poetically. Literally, Wendell Barry put words to all the feelings that I had, and Wendell and I spent a lot of time together in those days. And then there were people who were mentors in a very practical sense in business—old family connections who showed me the way.

Giving Back: In what ways did your personal leadership skills make a difference?

Gary Hirshberg: I have kind of patented the idea of questioning authority and challenging assumptions. In other words, I think there are a lot of people here who would credit me with helping them to see beyond the obvious. H. L. Mencken said that for every complex problem, there's an answer that's clear, simple, and wrong. I think if we had listened to all the business advisors and all the venture capitalists and all these know-it-all's from the early going, you and I would not be having this conversation because I wouldn't be here. We would have died an early and tragic and painful death. So I think asking this basic question, which I summarize in two words—Why not?—and getting other people to ask the same is my contribution.

Giving Back: How do you find people who routinely ask "Why not?"

Gary Hirshberg: Well, first of all, it's impossible to train that mind-set. It's something that people either have or don't have. I need to be honest here and tell you I've had a 25-year struggle with this and I think I'm still trying to figure it out. On the one hand, I know it's been what's put us on the map and what made us possible as a business. On the other hand, I know that sometimes the answer is "because it's done that way," and I've needed people who are more conservative or traditionally oriented to help me at times to face that. And so a lot of my best hires have been my opposites, people who were able to provide a conventional answer where I didn't have one. In general, what I have found is that I have benefited by having professionals around me who do know the way it's done and that gives us a surge. We would get a surge of growth from having the right people in the right positions.

Giving Back: Then what?

Gary Hirshberg: Then the inevitable next wave is that they run up against walls because organic food does cost more and we just don't compete on price that well. So you need to pull out the "Why not?" question again—my pendulum swings back and forth here. So it's a journey and it continues to be. In many respects I'm just a little bit further up the learning curve and I'm pretty humble about that.

Giving Back: Looking back, would you take a different approach?

Gary Hirshberg: I think the old adage that there is 20-20 vision in hindsight is, of course, true, and certainly I have no question that I wish I had done some things differently. Notably, I think we were a little bit overly optimistic with our early forecasts. I hired some people and I respected what I thought they knew, and learned later that they were just good talkers or just didn't know as much as I thought—that set us back. There are plenty of things I would do differently but, in terms of overall method, the answer is "no." The irony is that going at these social problems through enterprise, and also by inventing new solutions where they didn't exist, ultimately guaranteed our independence. Danone has shocked the world with the level of independence I have, even though they own 85% of the company. I am completely running this company like I was the day we started it, and that wouldn't have happened if we hadn't struggled along the way. Now, similarly, you could say, "Well, gee, maybe if you hadn't struggled, you wouldn't have had to sell the majority of the company to Danone to provide an exit for your shareholders." But I'm into the next iteration now, which is bringing our business to scale and there's nothing like working with the fifth largest food company in the world to learn about scale. So I have no regrets.

Giving Back: How do you interest people in joining with you in your efforts?

Gary Hirshberg: We just created a nonprofit this year. I could call it the culmination of my life's work—if it doesn't sound too pretentious—in the sense that I went into this thing as an academic. I studied and started to do my thesis work and eventually realized that I needed to study the *solutions* to the problems of climate change, not just the problems. That first led me to the nonprofit world which, in turn, led me to business, because I came to realize that most problems exist because business hasn't made the solutions a priority. I've come to realize that through our conscious consumption we can really change the way business is run. People think that they are the recipients of what business offers, but really they've got it all wrong. Business spends billions of dollars to tally up what consumers' interests are and is absolutely fixed on meeting those interests. So we created a nonprofit called Climate Counts, which scores the largest consumer companies in the world on their climate performance and lets people know what the scores are. So, through their conscious consumption or just through text messaging, they can get a note off to Bill Gates or Steve Jobs to say, "You know what, I'm going to buy an iPod this time, but your score concerns me and I might not buy another one the next time unless you've improved." I call it doing aikido with commerce. Commerce is very destructive, but if you can take the thrust and redirect it, I think that there are ways to get people on board even if they're not fully conscious that that's what you're doing.

Giving Back: Any corporate executives right now you admire for how they're giving back to the community?

Gary Hirshberg: The easy one that always comes to my lips is Yvon Chouinard at Patagonia. He's a friend and also a real hero of mine. I just think he's really on track. He's still committed to the grass roots. First of all, they've consciously altered their product lines to walk the talk and have been very conscious of the kinds of business practices that I think are needed to model twenty-first-century behaviors. Like us, they give many, many, many grants to small environmental networks, and—Margaret Mead was right—that's still the way you change things, I think, on a big scale.[2]

Giving Back: What is the personal philosophy that energizes and motivates you today?

Gary Hirshberg: Someone once said, "Anyone who thinks they're too small to make a difference has never been in bed with a mosquito." I use that in my upcoming book [*Stirring It Up: How to Make Money and Save the World* (Hyperion, 2008)] and I really believe it. I just think we can all make a huge difference. I really believe in the power of one.

Giving Back: How do you measure your own success in achieving your goals, both business and personal?

Gary Hirshberg: Obviously, number one, we measure it in classical business terms. How are we faring against the status quo? But we also consider the number of family farmers we're buying from and, coincidentally, the number of acres that we're supporting. At the end of the day, if I have to write my epitaph and put a stake in the ground, that's going to be the one true measure of whether we actually did something: Have more farmers survived? Have more farmers prospered? Have more acres remained in agriculture and organic than before? It's too hard to measure global temperature changes as a direct result of Stonyfield's activities, but we can measure the number of farmers who have survived and prospered, and we can measure the number of acres of land that have remained in agriculture and organic.

NOTES

1. Gary Hirshberg, "Profits with a Conscience,"*Leader to Leader,* Winter 2002, p. 24
2. The complete quotation from Margaret Mead is: "Never doubt that a small group that a small group of thoughtful, committed citizens can change the world. Indeed, it's the only thing that ever has."

CHAPTER 8

SPORTS for San Diego's Exceptional Athletes

Let me win. But if I cannot win, let me be brave in the attempt.

—SPECIAL OLYMPICS ATHLETE OATH

On March 12, 2007, the Special Olympics of Southern California (SOSC)—led by president and CEO Bill Shumard—announced the closing of the San Diego County Special Olympics office, the suspension with pay of the office's four staff members pending an investigation into "irregularities," and the cancellation of the San Diego annual basketball tournament, an event that routinely attracted more than 500 Special Athletes from across Southern California. With these events, a social earthquake of unprecedented proportions was triggered within San Diego's disabled sports community, eventually leading to the founding of a new nonprofit athletic organization for people with disabilities aged 5 through adult: SPORTS for Exceptional Athletes (S4EA).

The Special Olympics is perhaps the preeminent organization serving disabled athletes anywhere in the world. Founded in 1968 by Eunice Kennedy Shriver, the organization boasts the active worldwide participation of more than 2.25 million athletes and 500,000 volunteer coaches in more than 150 countries.[1] In San Diego, the Special Olympics program was founded in 1969, and numbers more than 1,000 disabled athlete participants.[2]

When Peter Economy first learned about the San Diego County Special Olympics program, his oldest son Peter was already 16 years old. However, the younger Peter was quickly drawn into the Special Olympics basketball league, coached by San Diego's director Walter Jackson and Myra Snowdall. The athletes played hard and they played well, and Peter—who, despite his disabilities, is a skilled and aggressive athlete himself—was quickly welcomed into the group. Born with a rare genetic disorder—tuberous sclerosis, which caused a variety of ailments, ranging from epilepsy to tumors to learning delays—Peter's love of basketball found its true fruition in the 2006 San Diego basketball tournament. It was at this tournament, which drew teams—and hundreds of athletes— from across southern California that he spent his very first night away from his parents, and began to get a sense that there was an exciting life ahead of him as an independent adult.

The elder Peter Economy—a full-time writer, and chairman and CEO of his own company—has long been in the world of business, first as a contract negotiator, then as an administrative and project manager. Peter had long dabbled in the world of nonprofits and community-based organizations—he has written a couple of books for nonprofit leaders (*Enterprising Nonprofits* [John Wiley & Sons, 2001] and *Strategic Tools for Social Entrepreneurs* [John Wiley & Sons, 2002]), serves as associate editor for *Leader to Leader* magazine (the mission of the Leader to Leader Institute is to strengthen leadership of the social sector), worked for a time for the San Diego Housing Commission, and has made numerous contributions of both time and money to nonprofits over the years, including schools, churches, scouting programs, and more. The last thing on his mind was helping to found a new community-based nonprofit organization.

That is, until the cancellation of the basketball tournament.

When the tournament was canceled, the San Diego Special Olympics community—the athletes, coaches, volunteers, and staff, many of whom had been with the program for 10, 20, and even 30 years or more—was thrown into complete and utter disarray. Peter Economy's son—and hundreds of other Special Athletes—had been anxiously anticipating the tournament for months. News of its cancellation, and of the closing of the San Diego County Special Olympics office and suspension of their programs, left leaders confused and hurt the participants. News in the immediate aftermath of this event was sketchy at best, limited to newspaper reports and a flurry of phone calls from coaches to parents, volunteers, and athletes—all wondering exactly what had happened to bring about this chain of events.

But, while the March 17 basketball tournament was canceled, a large group of Special Olympians and their supporters decided to gather that Saturday morning at the University of San Diego tournament site anyway to protest the decision to cancel the tournament and to demand answers from SOSC officials. Some who showed up weren't there to protest—they hadn't yet gotten word of the tournament cancellation. Participants carried hastily drawn signs supporting the athletes, and asking the questions, "Where's Walter?" and "Where's Clara?," referring to Walter Jackson and Clara Downes, the suspended director and assistant director, respectively, of the San Diego County Special Olympics. As it turned out, as a part of their suspension, Walter and Clara and the other two staffers were prohibited from interacting in any way with Special Olympians, causing them to have to stay away from events like this. A public address system was hastily set up, and a number of athletes, coaches, volunteers, and parents spoke to the assembled group, all expressing their confusion about SOSC's actions, their support for the suspended local Special Olympics leadership and staff, and their desire for the games to continue.

By this time, the cancellation of the tournament and closing of the San Diego office had landed on the radar screens of the local television news media, and several channels also showed up to report on the impromptu protest. Despite the protest, the decision to cancel the tournament was final, and SOSC decided to keep mum about the reasons behind it, and about the closing of the San Diego office and suspension of staff. And just like thousands of other parents of San Diego Special Olympians, and coaches and volunteers—and the athletes themselves—Peter Economy was left in the dark.

At the time, Peter and the others assumed that the SOSC would quickly fix what was broken. If San Diego staff was doing something wrong, then corrections would be made quickly, explanations and apologies would be offered, and the office would be reopened to business as usual. However, this was not the case. Corrections were not made by SOSC, explanations and apologies were not offered, and the office remained padlocked. For San Diego's Special Olympics community, this situation demanded answers and it demanded action, but neither were forthcoming from SOSC headquarters. This leadership vacuum needed to be filled, and it soon became apparent to Peter—and many others within the San Diego Special Olympics community—that it would be up to them to take action if there was going to be any hope of returning to the status quo. But exactly what this action might be—and what status quo they would be returning—was still unclear.

Within a couple of days after the March 17 protest, word was passed through the grapevine that there would be a meeting of interested volunteers, coaches, and parents to discuss the situation and to start developing strategies for trying to work with the SOSC to get the San Diego program back on track. A local realtor—Eddy Dunkel—offered a conference room in his office as a meeting place for this first meeting and for the others that followed. Slowly—after much discussion—a consensus began to emerge: that the group needed answers from SOSC as to why they closed the San Diego office and suspended Walter Jackson and Clara Downes and the other local staff, and that if these answers were not forthcoming from Bill Shumard or other SOSC leaders, that the group would need to appeal to the board of directors of the SOSC and to the national organization, up to and including Tim Shriver—Eunice Shriver's son and chairman of Special Olympics.

Peter Economy attended these sessions and wondered what he could do to help. Sure, he could attend the meetings, and provide his point of view and emotional support to the other parents, athletes, coaches, and volunteers, but it didn't seem like much of a contribution to him. However, it soon became clear that there was a role that Peter could take on—helping to facilitate communication within San Diego's Special Olympics community. Since the San Diego staff was under a gag order from the SOSC, the normal communication links had been shut down. What the community needed was a place to keep in touch with the latest developments, to rally together, and to know that there were others like them who cared about saving the program.

Years before, Peter had taught himself how to build his own web site using Microsoft FrontPage. The site (www.petereconomy.com), while simple, was sufficient for his needs. He had also recently been helping out with the blog for Dr. J. Robert Beyster—the founder of Science

Applications International Corporation—with whom he had recently coauthored a book, *The SAIC Solution* (John Wiley & Sons, 2007). So Peter decided to create a blog for the San Diego Special Olympics community, using Google's Blogger service (www.blogger.com). This blog—which was active from March 23 through May 8, 2007—can still be found at www.s4ea.blogspot.com. Soon, Peter found himself in the middle of a whirlwind of communications as he compiled and listed newspaper and television news reports on the San Diego Special Olympics woes, reprinted letters to the editor from the *San Diego Union-Tribune* and other local newspapers, and provided names and email addresses of SOSC board members for the public to contact to register their concerns with San Diego's situation.

Here is Peter's first post to the blog:

Save Our Special Olympics

My son, Peter, is a Special Olympian with an intense love for sports. The annual San Diego Special Olympics Basketball Tournament in which he was to play on March 17 and 18—along with his teammates, and 47 other teams from around Southern California—was abruptly canceled and the San Diego office shut down on March 13, 2007, by Bill Shumard, president and chief executive officer of the Special Olympics of Southern California.

This blog is a gathering place for supporters of San Diego County Special Olympics—volunteers, coaches, parents, sponsors, and the Olympians themselves. It is a place to keep up to date, to share information, and to learn what we can do to help save our very special program.

Thank you for joining us.

The initial ad-hoc group of concerned coaches, volunteers, and parents meeting at Eddy Dunkel's office quickly metamorphosed into a more formal organization, providing leadership and direction in the leadership vacuum left by the SOSC. The media needed people in the San Diego Special Olympics community to talk to, and Peter and others volunteered to be available for interviews. And when the group decided to organize a Community Forum to update athletes and the community on the latest news, Peter volunteered to present a list of demands to the public—demands that would be forwarded to the SOSC.

When Peter arrived at the Fraternal Order of Eagles hall in the Hillcrest neighborhood of San Diego at 6:00 PM on March 29, the building was surrounded by television news vans, cameras, and reporters from all the major networks, and parking was so scarce that he had to park five blocks away. The hall was filled—standing room only—with hundreds of athletes, coaches, volunteers, and parents, all waiting for answers yet to be provided by the SOSC, and filled with a burning desire to express their outrage over the cancellation of the basketball tournament and suspension of Walter, Clara, and the other members of the local staff.

Many long-time members of the San Diego Special Olympics community rose to give speeches, and to express their personal hurt and confusion over the events that had transpired. Unfortunately, though invited to attend, no representatives from the SOSC were there to hear them. And although it had been many years since Peter had made a speech to a group this large—numbering more than 300 people—he faced down his nerves and presented the group's demands:

> We, the athletes, coaches, parents, volunteers, donors, and community supporters of San Diego County Special Olympics (SDCSO) are outraged. We are all deeply committed to SDCSO and have invested countless hours throughout the years making our program one of the best in the world. We feel that the actions of the Special Olympics Southern California (SOSC) staff over the past few weeks, and the past few years, are jeopardizing the future of the program. We are deeply concerned that their actions are taking our program in a direction we cannot support and feel that we must act now to protect not only our program in San Diego, but the Special Olympics programs throughout Southern California. Therefore, we request the following actions be taken by the Special Olympics Southern California Board of Directors and by Special Olympics International:
>
> **1. We would like answers.**
>
> We would like to know who allegedly reported the "concerns" regarding the SDCSO staff, what specifically those concerns were, when they were reported, and to whom they were reported. We want to know specifically what has been investigated, how many people have been interviewed, who they were, and what their findings have been. We, as

integral participants in the program, would like the opportunity to be interviewed as well.

2. We want an investigation of SOSC by Special Olympics International.

We would like a review of the past several years to identify the impact that SOSC policy changes have had on Special Olympics athletes. We want to know the number of programs in Southern California, the number of athletes in each program, the number of sports offered, and the number of tournaments held by each area. We would also like to know the number of athletes/teams at hosted tournaments. We want to know how the budget has changed, the number of staff members at SOSC and their salaries. We want to know the percentage of the Special Olympic budget that has been spent on SOSC staff and office support salaries over the past few years. We want to see concrete numbers regarding areas that have undergone restructuring. We want an accounting of the number of coaches/volunteers which have been fired and the reasoning behind these firings.

3. We want representation.

We feel that athletes, families and volunteers should have a real voice in the running of our program and want increased representation at the SOSC office. We want to have a vote on the "reorganization" proposed for our area. We want to be a working and voting part of the Board of Directors at the state and local levels throughout California. We want to have representation when deciding on policies that directly affect athletes, coaches and when hiring the people who will administrate our programs. We want the people who participate in the program each week to be given a meaningful voice in running it.

4. EFFECTIVE IMMEDIATELY—without prejudice, we want Walter Jackson and Clara Downes restored to their positions as the Area Director and the Assistant Area Director of San Diego County Special Olympics.

Historically, Walter Jackson and Clara Downes have successfully run the SDCSO program with the athlete's best interest at heart. We have full confidence that they will continue to do so. We also feel that a paid

Area Director and Assistant Area Director are vital positions, given the size and scope of the programs offered in San Diego versus the proposed model.

5. Removal of SOSC Staff.

We feel that Bill Shumard, Jan Palchikoff, and other SOSC staff members, have disregarded the needs and feelings of athletes, parents, coaches, volunteers, donors, and community supporters, which is in fact a direct conflict of their Mission Statement. Therefore, the SOSC officers and staff should be terminated from their positions within the organization. We feel that superior and appropriate officers and staff members can be found who truly want to serve the athletes, the families, the coaches, the donors, and the community supporters that are already dedicated to and involved in our organization.

By this time, the SOSC and national Special Olympics offices were being bombarded with a daily barrage of letters and email messages in support of Walter and Clara, and demanding answers. But despite this outpouring of support for the San Diego program and leadership team, the SOSC remained mum, while the national organization threw its support firmly behind Bill Shumard and the SOSC. Finally, five weeks after the cancellation of the basketball tournament and closure of the San Diego County Special Olympics office, Bill Shumard scheduled a meeting in San Diego with a select group of 30 representatives of the San Diego Special Olympics community. Slated to attend on behalf of the SOSC were key members of their leadership team, including members of the SOSC board of directors and executives and managers, and a couple of representatives from Special Olympics North America.

By the time of this meeting—held on April 16—the San Diego group had come to the realization that simply fixing the broken situation with the Special Olympics organization was becoming increasingly unlikely, and that creating a new organization—either within the Special Olympics organization, or outside of it—might be the only way to achieve the group's goals. These goals had been refined into a new set of three demands to be presented by long-time Special Olympics coach Greg Ahrens at the meeting:

Keeping in mind the best interests of our San Diego special athletes, we make the following three demands:

1. We demand the reinstatement of Walter Jackson and Clara Downes and resignations of Bill Shumard and Jan Palchikoff.
2. In the alternative, allow San Diego and nearby areas to establish its own Special Olympics chapter.
3. If one of the two above demands are not met, we are prepared to form an alternative sports program to meet the needs of our athletes.

Unfortunately, the meeting did not go well. Here is Peter Economy's summary of the meeting from the Save Our Special Olympics blog:

Oh, well . . .

I had hoped that Special Olympics Southern California (SOSC) would wave its magic wand at tonight's meeting between representatives of the San Diego County Special Olympics community and bigwigs from Special Olympics North America (SONA) and SOSC and make everything all better.

Unfortunately, there was no magic wand, and things are not all better.

Yes. The reps from SONA and SOSC put on a terrific performance. They set up the meeting (complete with a carefully selected list of attendees, and a hired security guard to enforce it), aggressively controlled the agenda, and brought in some big guns, including SOSC board of directors chair Pat McClenahan, board of governors chair Rafer Johnson, and president Bill Shumard. They provided scripted answers to a long list of "concerns" culled from email messages, letters, and media interviews. They asked if we had additional concerns that were not on their list—and they even answered a few of those.

However, the answers to two key questions since Day One—"Where are Walter and Clara?" and "Why was the San Diego office shut down?"—were not answered.

Throughout the presentation, the message was loud and clear: The program isn't changing for you, so you had better get with the program.

Said McClenahan about SOSC's current regime, "This is the most talented staff that we have ever employed. The board is 100 percent behind this staff. This board is fully apprised and we support the staff." This is the same message we have gotten on up the line, all the way to the top of the Special Olympics International hierarchy.

This despite the fact that this "most talented staff" made the grave error of shutting down the San Diego County Special Olympics office and cancelling the annual basketball tournament—an error that had a profoundly negative impact on our athletes and which SOSC now admits it should not have made. And, ultimately, that is what it is all about—the athletes—and providing them with the very best athletic experience possible.

As the meeting ended—and after a spirited presentation of petitions signed by 692 supporters of San Diego Special Olympics, and demands for Walter and Clara to be reinstated, and for Bill Shumard and Jan Palchikoff to step down (made by our very gutsy representative Greg [Ahrens])—I was left with the sad realization that neither SONA nor SOSC offered us anything of substance in tonight's meeting. No list of action items for follow up, no invitation to join in SOSC's decision-making process, no local voice in how the San Diego Special Olympics program will be run, no guarantee that our office won't be shut down again, or more events cancelled at the last minute—leaving us all in the dark, wondering what happened.

But, then again, why should they offer us anything? As Dan McCarthy, one of SONA's directors of development pointed out several times during the course of the meeting, the San Diego County Special Olympics program does not belong to us—to San Diego's talented, dedicated, and hardworking athletes, coaches, volunteers, parents, sponsors, and donors.

Oh, well . . .

It was ultimately this realization that the San Diego Special Olympics program did not belong to the San Diego Special Olympics community that constituted the straw that broke the proverbial camel's back. If the program wasn't theirs—if SOSC didn't want the community's input or participation in helping to try to fix what was broken and make it better—then why should they try to save it? So, based on the outcome of the meeting, the group decided to move forward with its own organization. This new organization—SPORTS for Exceptional Athletes—was incorporated just five weeks after the date of the cancelled basketball tournament. The elder Peter was asked to join the board of directors as vice president—an offer that he readily accepted—and Walter Jackson and Clara Downes were hired by the board to run the new organization as executive director and associate director. SPORTS for Exceptional Athletes ended up attracting many of the San Diego County Special

Olympics athletes, coaches, and volunteers—quickly eclipsing the old organization, which even today struggles to continue operations.

As the stories in this book so graphically illustrate, there are an unlimited number of different ways that you can give back to your community. You don't have to be rich or famous, you don't have to be a CEO, and you don't have to belong to any particular organization. You simply have to have a heartfelt desire to change the world around you, and be willing to invest some time to help. In Peter Economy's case, giving back meant being willing to take time to help—applying his writing skills and knowledge of web site and blog technology, attending organizational meetings, and stepping up into leadership positions when there was a need for him to do so.

Today, SPORTS for Exceptional Athletes is a healthy and thriving organization that serves hundreds of San Diegans with developmental disabilities. As the organization's legacy grows, Peter will look back proudly on the role he played in the events that led to its founding. Instead of simply writing a check, Peter gave something much more valuable to his community: his time and his leadership skills and his technical knowledge. And, as it turned out, these contributions were worth far more than any check he could have written.

Q&A with Peter Economy, Vice President of SPORTS for Exceptional Athletes (San Diego, California)

Giving Back: What event(s) took place that prodded you to decide you wanted to give back?

Peter Economy: I have long felt a desire to help others in my community in any way I could, which because of my busy schedule, never seemed like enough. When the Special Olympics Southern California (SOSC) canceled the annual San Diego basketball tournament—which my son had been anxiously anticipating for months—and closed the San Diego office, I, along with many others, took it very personally. I vowed to do whatever was necessary to help fix the local Special Olympics program. When it became clear that this would not be possible, I personally committed to help start a new, locally controlled athletic organization for people with developmental disabilities—devoting hundreds of hours to achieving this goal.

Giving Back: How old were you at the time?

Peter Economy: I was 51 years old.

Giving Back: Did you have friends and/or acquaintances who discouraged you?

Peter Economy: No. Everyone I spoke to about our problems with the SOSC—especially within my family and within the San Diego Special Olympics community—was very supportive. We were getting lots of attention in the local press, and people I talked to who had no connection at all to the disabled community were aware of the situation and very encouraging.

Giving Back: What is the most significant contribution you have made with your leadership skills?

Peter Economy: I was part of the team of concerned coaches, volunteers, and parents of Special Olympians who helped chart a course to creating our own nonprofit athletic organization dedicated to serving mentally disabled San Diegans, ages five and up—SPORTS for Exceptional Athletes (S4EA). I volunteered to speak with the press, to lead key organizational meetings, and—when we finally established S4EA—I agreed to serve as vice president of the board of directors.

Giving Back: What is the most significant contribution you have made with your resources?

Peter Economy: The most significant contribution I made is without doubt my time and business expertise. As they say, time is money, and I have given much time to first trying to work with the Special Olympics organization, and then helping to design and charter a new nonprofit organization, SPORTS for Exceptional Athletes. I also spent countless hours setting up and maintaining the Save Our Special Olympics blog and then the S4EA web site. I put the web site together very late one night while on a business trip to Durango, Colorado, and it was up and running just in time for a mention in the *San Diego Union-Tribune* newspaper. My wife and

I also made a nice financial contribution to the organization's start-up.

Giving Back: What was the objective of your project, and whom did you wish to benefit?

Peter Economy: The initial objective was to restore the leadership and programs of the San Diego County Special Olympics office, which would benefit San Diego's large community of Special Olympics athletes. When we failed at that, our objective changed to starting up our own nonprofit athletic organization, and hiring the former leadership of the local Special Olympics office.

Giving Back: What changes, if any, would you make today in your initial approach? Why?

Peter Economy: I would make no changes in our approach. We first tried to work with the Special Olympics Southern California powers that be. When it became clear that they had no interest in working with us, then we moved quickly to take action to establish our own organization. We went from the closure of the San Diego office to incorporation and funding of our new nonprofit organization in only another five weeks which, in retrospect, was quite an accomplishment.

Giving Back: How do you interest people in working for a specific cause?

Peter Economy: I don't know that you interest people in working for a specific cause so much as you decide what your organization's mission is, and then do whatever it takes to be true to it. People who believe in your mission will be naturally attracted to your cause.

Giving Back: What corporate executive(s) do you admire most for their contributions (personal and philanthropic)?

Peter Economy: I personally admire executives who are low-key and unassuming about their own wealth, but who make dramatic contributions to their communities. Milton Hershey was one such corporate executive. He founded Hershey Chocolate as well as the Milton Hershey School. Dr. J. Robert Beyster—founder and former chairman and CEO of $8 billion+ science and engineering firm Science Applications International Corporation is another such corporate executive I admire for his contributions—primarily by founding organizations (the Beyster Institute, and the Foundation for Enterprise Development) that promote employee ownership and the American ideals of free enterprise and financial independence.

Giving Back: What societal need(s) are you most concerned about?

Peter Economy: I am personally most concerned about the needs of the millions of developmentally challenged Americans—both today, and tomorrow.

Giving Back: How can you become personally engaged in solutions?

Peter Economy: By finding a social need that gets you fired up so much that you have no choice other than diving in to help. No matter what it is—from building homes for the homeless, to leading youth programs, to making contributions to causes in which you believe—when you find the right cause, your passion will rise to meet it.

Giving Back: What is your personal philosophy that energizes and motivates you?

Peter Economy: To leave the world a better place than I found it.

Giving Back: How will you measure your success in accomplishing your purpose?

Peter Economy: By how I chose to live each day, and by the people whose lives I positively impact. I am still in charge of the S4EA web site. Each time we add a new practice, or a new sport, or a dance or other social activity for our athletes, I know that we have succeeded in the task that we set out to accomplish. And I feel good all over again.

Notes

1. www.specialolympics.org/Special+Olympics+Public+Website/English/Coach/ Coaching_Guides/Basics+of+Special+Olympics/Special+Olympics+History .htm.
2. www.specialolympicssandiego.com/MISSION.html.

CHAPTER 9

You Don't Have to be a CEO (or Have a Million Dollars) To Give Back to Your Community

It's easy to make a buck.
It's a lot tougher to make a difference.

—TOM BROKAW

Throughout this book, we have described examples of businesspeople who have given back—some to their neighborhoods, communities, and towns, and others to the world. A number of these men and women were in positions of great power within their organizations—founders, CEOs—and one or two had millions of dollars available to use to create their foundations and charitable nonprofits. However, a key point of this book is to show you that you don't have to be a CEO, and you don't have to have a lot of money to give back to your community. As the example of Kiva.org's Matt and Jessica Flannery shows, you just have to have passion; a good idea; and a lot of time, energy, and perseverance.

In this chapter, we provide a variety of examples of people of modest means who have found creative ways to give back to their communities, as well as companies that are finding innovative ways to help their people to give back. It's our hope that you'll be inspired by these stories, and that you'll commit to making a difference by giving back.

HILLEL KATZEFF AND THE FAMILY MICROFOUNDATION

A certified financial planner, and owner of HK Financial, Hillel Katzeff of San Diego, California, has recommended and helped set up various charitable giving structures—including charitable trusts, donor-advised funds, and family foundations—for a number of his well-off clients who were seeking tax benefits and an efficient way to make charitable donations to deserving nonprofits and community-based organizations. Unfortunately, these strategies are tools generally reserved only for those individuals and families with a lot of money, and very few people outside of that particular demographic have the means to use one of these structures.

Hillel wondered: What if families of modest means could also create foundations that would have an impact on their communities? Most individuals and families want to give back and make a difference but may not know how to do so as a family. He wanted to democratize family giving by using a family foundation structure, while at the same time reinforcing family bonds since the entire family is involved in the decision-making process and the giving experience.

And what if there were a way for families of similar interests to pool their foundations' resources to leverage the impact of their efforts?

After much thought and reflection, the idea came to Hillel: the family MicroFoundation™. According to Hillel, the collective voice of a family is captured in a MicroFoundation document that it develops over the course of several meetings. Similar to family foundations (but smaller and at no cost to establish), MicroFoundations allow families of any means to take immediate action on the causes they believe are important—as a family.

Once a family has chosen its goals (Hillel has also developed a unique tool for facilitating family group discussions, Our Little Blue Box™), the MicroFoundation can be established. Hillel suggests that a family think of its MicroFoundation as a statement of goals and dreams, and the family's action plan to attain them. Once established, a family can share the joy of accomplishment as they achieve over time what they set out to do in their MicroFoundation charter.

Following is a sample MicroFoundation charter from Hillel's website (www.familygiving.org):

CASESTUDY	THE SMITH FAMILY MICROFOUNDATION FOR LITERACY CHARTER

The Smith Family is dedicated to lifelong learning and education. We are dedicated to helping those children and adults in our community who need help learning how to read.

We will do this by attending a cultural event once a quarter (as a family) and volunteering (as a family) to promote literacy in our community with an existing not-for-profit organization. We also will visit or volunteer at our local public library.

Roles and Responsibilities During our family meetings we will discuss and agree on which cultural event to attend during the next three months. We will take turns to coordinate and organize these family events:

- Attend a fun play or musical event
- Support and/or volunteer at a book fair

Each family member will have discretion over the way they contribute to the family volunteer activities and may include:

- Collecting used books to be donated to the Literacy Center
- Volunteer at the Literacy Center or public library, i.e. teaching someone to read

Funding We do, or do not need to put some money in our MicroFoundation at this time. How much? When? From whom?

Naming The name of our MicroFoundation is: The Smith Family MicroFoundation for Literacy.

Meetings We will meet before dinner on the first Tuesday of each month for half an hour to plan our activities and discuss the progress we are making.

Board of Directors David, Jane, Brendan, Robin, and Lou Smith The Smith Family MicroFoundation for Literacy is Established as of Date

So, Hillel Katzeff figured out a way to give back to his community—and, indeed, to the world—in a way that was meaningful to him and that didn't cost a lot of money to implement. Hillel's latest idea is to establish listings of family MicroFoundations on his familygiving.org web site, along with a photo of each family and a brief summary of their MicroFoundation's goals. This would enable families with similar goals to communicate with one another with the aim of pooling their efforts and their financial resources—potentially multiplying their impact many times over. But this is in the future. For now, Hillel is very happy with the idea he has established, and he is working hard to publicize it and spread the idea—that the MicroFoundation allows *any* family to create a charitable organization that can focus their efforts and have a very real and lasting impact in their community.

KYLE ZIMMER AND FIRST BOOK

Before cofounding First Book—a nonprofit organization that distributes free books to underprivileged children—Kyle Zimmer was a self-described type triple-A corporate lawyer. That is, until she volunteered in 1991 to tutor a young boy in a Washington, D.C., soup kitchen. She had assumed that the tutoring program would have plenty of resources—books and the like—to use as instructional aids. Kyle soon found out that this assumption was incorrect. She also found that low-income children in general lack the books they need to learn how to read at their grade level. Says Zimmer, "When you look at the data, more than 60% of families who are at or below the poverty line don't have a single book in their home for their children. If you can imagine even trying to accomplish math when you can't read . . . it's utterly paralyzing, and they carry that paralysis straight into adulthood."[1]

So Kyle decided to do something about this problem, putting her legal career on hold and cofounding First Book in 1992 with fellow attorneys Peter Gold (who today serves as First Book's chairman) and Elizabeth Arky (who serves as a director on the organization's board). Today, Zimmer serves as president of First Book. The idea behind First Book was to create a national program that would accept and distribute to children in need a portion of the millions of unsold and surplus books that publishers destroy every year. The plan was to reach children through existing literacy programs in a variety of different settings, such as Head Start centers, libraries, soup kitchens, churches, housing projects, and after-school initiatives to transform the quality of preschool and after-school programs nationwide.

The new organization managed to distribute 12,000 books in three different communities during its first year of operation. However, in the years since, the growth of Zimmer's program has been stunning. Since 1992, First Book has distributed more than 50 million books to children in over 1,300 communities across the United States. But this extraordinary success story is not just about transferring lots of surplus books from publishers to children; it's about the impact that this program has on the lives of the children it touches—and on the communities in which they live. In a study funded by the U.S. Department of Education, Fund for the Improvement of Education, the Louis Harris organization surveyed 2,564 individuals over a 14-month period to determine the effectiveness of First Book's operating model. According to First Book's Web site (www.firstbook. org), the survey resulted in the following findings:

- *First Book works for children.* More than half of the children—55%—reported having an increased interest in reading. Additionally, the number of young people demonstrating a "high interest in reading" nearly tripled (increasing from 23% to 61%) after receiving books from First Book.
- *First Book works for local programs.* Seventy-eight percent of the mentors, administrators, and professionals running community-based tutoring and mentoring programs estimated that the "impact of First Book books on a child's desire to read" was "very important."
- *First Book works for the community.* The members of the First Book Local Advisory Boards surveyed were also overwhelmingly supportive of our efforts in their communities. 98% of them state that their community was "better off" because of First Book's work.[2]

In its early days, First Book simply accepted donations of surplus books from publishers, redistributing them to children in need. However, as time went on, First Book has commissioned special print runs of books from publishers at steep discounts. The First Book model has evolved into three distinct parts: First Book Advisory Boards, First Book Marketplace, and First Book National Book Bank. According to First Book, each of these parts plays an important role in success of the organization as a whole:

- **First Book Advisory Boards**, located in more than 260 communities in the United States, provide programs serving disadvantaged children the opportunity to purchase books from special catalogs offering thousands of quality children's book titles. A typical First Book Advisory Board grant lasts for one year and offers each child in the program a steady diet of books (usually one book per month), all at no cost to the children or the program. All First Book Advisory Board grant applications are reviewed at the local level by members of the Advisory Boards.
- **The First Book Marketplace** is an online store that enables programs serving children from low-income families to purchase children's books at deeply reduced prices. The Marketplace offers a broad range of high-quality and award-winning titles for children ages 0 to 18, including board books, picture books, novels, reference books, and bilingual titles. The average price for a Marketplace title is less than $1.80, including shipping and handling.
- **The First Book National Book Bank** distributes large quantities of publisher-donated brand-new books to programs serving children from low-income families. There are 25 to 30 book distributions hosted by the First Book National Book Bank annually at a variety of sites across the United States. The books are free to programs that are able to pick them up or just $0.25 per book to have them shipped. Because distributions are based on generous donations from our publishing partners, there is no set schedule or list of upcoming locations for book distributions. The First Book National Book Bank also coordinates First Book's response to the 2005 Gulf Region hurricanes, Book Relief.[3]

To provide additional resources for its programs, First Book has forged partnerships with Lincoln Mercury, Cheerios, the Walt Disney Company, Universal Studios, Time Warner Cable, and many other companies.

So does Kyle Zimmer ever look back wistfully at her job as a high-power corporate lawyer? Maybe. Or maybe not. Says Kyle, winner of the 2007 Outstanding Social Entrepreneur award from the Schwab Foundation for Social Entrepreneurship, "I have had unbelievably great experiences professionally. I'm not somebody who was bitter and stomped out of the private sector. Nonetheless, my experiences there never fully satisfied a part of me. I am now exhausted. Every day feels like you're playing four sets of tennis in the hot sun, but you go home feeling like you've played a great game."[4]

CHARLES BEST AND DONORSCHOOSE.ORG

In 2000, Bronx high school teacher Charles Best experienced firsthand the negative impact that a lack of teaching materials in his public school was having on students. On one hand, years of underfunding had led to widespread shortages of teaching supplies and resources in many public school systems. And on the other hand, what limited supplies and resources that were available were tightly controlled by decision makers at the top of the organization's administrative staffs, and doled out to teachers based on their own preferences, not necessarily based on the real needs of teachers and their students. As Charles explored this problem in more detail, he felt certain that there was an untapped potential in people who were frustrated by their lack of influence over the use of their charitable donations. Charles wondered, "What if there were a simple way to provide students with the books, technology, and supplies that they need to learn?" and, further, "What if people from all walks of life could connect directly with public schools, learn about specific classroom needs, and choose how to help?"

The answer to these questions was an entirely new approach to getting necessary teaching materials and resources into the classrooms that most needed them: a web site that would serve as a "middle man," that is, that would match teachers who needed teaching materials and resources with potential donors who wanted to help by using their good old-fashioned cash for the specific projects that they personally believed would have the greatest impact. Rather than making a general contribution to a school that would use it as the school's *administrators* pleased, Charles Best's paradigm-busting idea was to let the donors themselves decide how their money would be used.

DonorsChoose.org is the result of Best's brainstorm—a web site that brings together teachers with specific needs with donors who want to give back to their communities by providing the funding that these teachers need. Says Charles, "People on the front lines have the best ideas for how to improve things. We really are based on this idea that teachers have all this pent-up classroom expertise, and that if we could just empower them to come up with microsolutions, they're going to come up with smarter ideas than anybody would at the top."[5]

So Charles had an idea, but he was a math teacher, not a web site designer, and he didn't know anything about putting together the DonorsChoose.org site. So he drew the design of the home page on a piece of paper, then paid a programmer in Poland $1,500 to build the site. Once the site was up and running, Charles was faced with his biggest hurdle: How to get teachers to visit and submit proposals, and how to get donors to visit and send in their money. As Charles found out, this was much easier said than done. After bribing a group of teachers in his school with dessert, he convinced eleven of them to submit proposals, which included projects for Immigration Novels ($200) and Baby Think-It-Over Dolls for Pregnancy Prevention ($400).

With the teacher side of the equation solved for now, Charles needed to find donors—and fast! He didn't have any rich friends or family members, but his aunt funded the very first project, and Charles himself anonymously funded the other ten. Now that the organization was gradually moving forward, Charles enlisted a group of student volunteers who met after school to assemble and address letters about DonorsChoose.org and inviting the recipients to participate.

After working at this task for three months—and sending out 2,000 letters, to addresses culled from Charles's high school and college alumni directories—$30,000 in donations arrived. While it was a lot of money, it still wasn't enough to make the organization self-sustaining. Things were getting desperate. Out of the blue—and after striking out with local reporters—Charles cold-called Jonathan Alter, a senior editor at *Newsweek* magazine, who, although he didn't know Charles, took the call. As it turned out, the editor didn't just take the call, he ended up writing a column for the magazine in which he claimed that DonorsChoose.org would "change the face of philanthropy." Oprah Winfrey read the piece and invited

Charles to appear on her show. That *Newsweek* article—and Oprah's attention—brought in a flood of donations that provided DonorsChoose with the funds it needed to become a fully self-sustaining organization.

The organization's mission is straightforward:

CASESTUDY   **OUR MISSION**

DonorsChoose is dedicated to addressing the scarcity and inequitable distribution of learning materials and experiences in our public schools. We believe this inequity is rooted in the following factors:

1. Shortages of learning materials prevent thorough, engaging instruction;
2. Top-down distribution of materials stifles our best teachers and discourages them from developing targeted solutions for their students; and
3. Small, directed contributions have gone un-tapped as a source of funding.

DonorsChoose will improve public education by engaging citizens in an online marketplace where teachers describe and individuals can fund specific student projects. We envision a nation where students in every community have the resources they need to learn.

The process begins when teachers submit proposals for the funding of specific projects or teaching resources or equipment—anything from dictionaries for at-home use ($259), to disposable cameras for a photography project to a geological field trip ($2,000). The DonorsChoose staff screens the proposals and then posts them on the DonorsChoose.org web site. When a proposal is funded, DonorsChoose purchases the items and then ships them directly to the teacher who requested them—along with a disposable camera with which to record the results and send back to DonorsChoose. DonorsChoose's staff compiles student thank-you notes, photographs, and a teacher impact letter and forwards them to the donor, who is able to monitor the progress of the project via his or her DonorsChoose online account. And like Kiva.org—described in detail in Chapter 3—DonorsChoose is primarily funded by voluntary contributions that donors give above and beyond their classroom donations. In fact, 93% of the thousands of DonorsChoose contributors have decided to give an extra 15% donation to fund the nonprofit's operations.[6]

Since its humble beginnings eight years ago, more than 28,000 individuals in all 50 states have made more than 62,000 donations totaling more than $14 million to support teacher proposals on DonorsChoose. org. According to DonorsChoose surveys, 75% of donors to the site are first-time givers to public schools. To date, more than 26,000 teachers in 7,300 different public schools have submitted more than 60,000 project proposals for their students, most of whom live in low-income communities. Resources provided by DonorsChoose—72% of which are reused by next year's students—break down as follow:

- Classroom supplies: 45%
- Books: 25%
- Technology: 17%
- Other resources: 7%
- Field trips: 5%
- Class visitors: 1%

Here is a sample proposal for funding submitted to DonorsChoose.org by a teacher at P.S. 11 Kathryn M. Phelan School in Woodside (Queens), New York:

CASESTUDY   FAMILY MATH NIGHT

I am currently a Math Coach in Woodside, Queens. I work in a K-6 school. The school is large and has approximately 1,300 students. I would like to hold a Family Math Night for the students in grades K-6 and their families.

This is a fun way to show the students and their parents that math is important! Since our school is large, the Family Math Night will be held on two different nights. The Family Math Night is an opportunity for students to play math games with their families. Not only will the students have fun playing the games, but they will be practicing math skills at the same time. The parents will have an opportunity to play the games their children play in class. They will also receive a copy of the game directions so they can help their child at home.

This is a wonderful opportunity to provide parents with the tools they need to help their children. After all, the Home-School connection is extremely important. In order to fulfill my goal, I will need dice, cards, glue sticks, cardstock, and pencils that say *I Love Math*. I do want the students to experience a Family Math Night and to experience a love for math!

The cost of the Math Materials is $856, including shipping and fulfillment.

With just a unique idea and a lot of passion and hard work, Charles Best and the DonorsChoose team have made tremendous strides in a relatively short amount of time. Perhaps it is no surprise that Best has attracted the attention—and support—of people and organizations such as Oprah Winfrey, the *New York Times*, Bank of America, J. P. Morgan Chase, Yahoo!, and many more. DonorsChoose has grown from serving the Bronx to serving schools in Chicago; Los Angeles; the San Francisco Bay Area; Washington, D.C.; and the entire states of Alabama, Indiana, Louisiana, Mississippi, New York, North Carolina, South Carolina, and Texas. The eventual goal? To serve every public school in the country. And—at the rate they are going—there is no doubt that they will one day achieve this goal, and perhaps even exceed it.

Notes

1. "Giving the Gift of Reading," CBS News, September 10, 2004.
2. www.firstbook.org/site/c.lwKYJ8NVJvF/b.674339/k.B71/Our_Impact.htm (accessed August 10, 2007).
3. http://register.firstbook.org/ (accessed August 10, 2007).
4. Hannah Storm, "Book 'em," *USA Weekend,* September 12, 2004.
5. Bill Blakemore, "Schoolkids Get What Donors Choose," ABC News, May 26, 2007.
6. Jonathan Alter, "Want to Buy My Students a $392 Camcorder? A Nonprofit Uses the Web to Work Marketplace Magic," Slate.com, February 16, 2007.

CHAPTER 10

And Just in Case You *Are* the CEO

*You get the best out of others
when you give the best of yourself.*

—Harvey S. Firestone

Of course, if you *are* the CEO, that can be a good thing, and it can help you open doors that might be closed to others. As a CEO, executive, or company owner, you can initiate and foster relationships with your counterparts in the community, you can direct human, financial, and other company resources to support specific nonprofits or community projects, and you can use your position—and your voice—to inspire others to join with you in your efforts. And, of course, you can personally give back to your community.

Remember that, as a leader, you set the example for the men and women who work for you. But, not only do you set an example for your employees, you also help to create your company's values as well as the overall environment in which your employees work. Truth be told, people prefer to work for organizations that are perceived to be more socially responsible than those that are perceived to be less socially responsible. And they are willing to vote this preference with their feet.

THE RESEARCH

According to research on 18- to 26-year-olds, companies that help their employees volunteer their professional skills to nonprofit organizations have a distinct advantage when it comes to recruiting new talent. Almost two-thirds of the respondents (62 percent) in the 2007 Volunteer IMPACT survey by Deloitte & Touche USA said they would prefer to work for companies that give them opportunities to contribute their talents to nonprofit organizations. Says Stan Smith, national director of Next Generation Initiatives for Deloitte & Touche USA, "This generation expects to make a difference. They give of themselves and they want their employers to help them contribute as well. Companies that facilitate meaningful community involvement opportunities for their people will be very attractive employers."[1]

This result echoes an earlier study by the Council on Foundations, which in 2001 sponsored a corporate philanthropy research initiative with Walker Information, Inc. According to the study—which included input from 2,400 businesses with 50 or more employees—a company's community engagement activities have a positive effect on the average employee's satisfaction and loyalty. The study also found that employee volunteering is a major factor in favorably influencing employee perceptions of the company, and that this factor consistently outweighs other related factors such as cash donations, in-kind contributions, and nonprofit sponsorship.[2]

In "Conversations with Disbelievers"—a paper published by the Ford Foundation—John Weiser and Simon Zadek cite a Council on Foundations/Walker Information research finding when they pointed out that, "A company's support of employee volunteerism is a key driver directly influencing employees' feelings about their jobs. For example, employees involved in employer-sponsored community events were 30% more likely to want to continue working for that company and help it be a success."[3]

What's particularly interesting about company efforts to be more socially responsible is that the positive impacts on organizations are quite broad and widespread—not narrowly focused. For example, a joint study by the Points of Light Foundation and the Center for Corporate Citizenship at Boston College found that employee volunteer programs can have a positive impact on companies in three areas.

Develop Employees

An employee volunteer program provides an opportunity for employees to:

- Demonstrate an interest in and ability for taking on new and different responsibilities
- Broaden skill sets
- Get noticed by management and become "promotable"
- Build competencies through an employment-related volunteer activity

Improve Public Perception

An employee volunteer program provides an opportunity for the company to:

- Improve brand recognition and corporate reputation
- Maintain positive perceptions
- Be a "good neighbor in the community"
- Meet expectations that the company is "involved in communities where . . . employees live and work"

Enhance Operations

An employee volunteer program provides opportunities to:

- Bring together staffers across job functions to develop projects
- Highlight messaging regarding the company's ability to "provide service to customers and the community"
- Improve cross-functional relationships
- Offer "high potential" leadership and project management skills
- Build client relationships[4]

Long story short, by setting a good example of corporate social responsibility within their companies, and by promoting socially responsible values and activities such as volunteerism, leaders can help their organizations do a better job of attracting talented new employees, and increasing employee satisfaction and retention. And, when given the option to leave their employer for a new job, they will tend to want to stay—even given the prospect of a higher salary—when their current employer is perceived to be more socially responsible than the prospective one.

LEADERS GIVING BACK

Of course, there are almost as many ways for leaders to give back as there are stars in the sky on a clear night in June. Some leaders create foundations, others promote volunteerism—and give employees time off to volunteer in their communities. Yet others are highly active and engaged in creating new kinds of socially responsible organizations. Here are a number of examples of CEOs, executives, and entrepreneurs who have found inspiring—and effective—ways to give back to their communities.

James Kenefick

James Kenefick is a long-time entrepreneur with a strong track record of success in building high tech, nutrition, and telecommunications businesses. As a CEO, James grew three separate businesses from $0 to 15 million, $0 to 30 million, and $0 to 75 million in revenues—all within ten years—and he has garnered a number of awards and honors as a result of his sharp business acumen, including twice being named an Ernst & Young Entrepreneur of the Year finalist, international board member of the Entrepreneur's Organization (EO), board member of the Washington D.C. chapter of the Young President's Organization (YPO), and serving on the Kauffman Foundation CEL Advisory Board.

While building these successful businesses was immensely satisfying to James, he knew that there was more to life than simply building businesses and making money. This belief came sharply into focus one dark day in September, 2001. Says Kenefick, "After 9/11, I had an epiphany—I realized that life is all about the journey, not the destination." Soon afterwards, James founded three new businesses, all with a bent towards social responsibility and giving back:

- **Working Excellence Capital Partners (WEX Capital) (http://www.wexcapitalpartners.com),** a merchant bank dedicated to sustainable, socially responsible investments, with a focus on sustainable/socially responsible emerging companies seeking $2 to 8 million in growth capital.
- **Working Excellence (http://www.workingexcellence.com),** an executive coaching and management consulting firm dedicated to helping CEOs, corporate boards, and executive teams achieve

and sustain high growth, increased productivity, and balance—in a socially conscious manner.

- **BetterWorld Telecom (http://betterworldtelecom.com),** which delivers local, long distance, Internet access, and Voice over Internet Protocol (VOIP) services to socially minded organizations throughout the United States—at rates 28% below the "big three" telecom firms.

BetterWorld Telecom is a particularly good example of how James now combines his entrepreneurial abilities with socially responsible business practices. At the very heart of the company is commitment to a triple bottom line: people, planet, profits, and a dedication to making the world a better place. To this end, BetterWorld Telecom donates 3% of its top-line revenues to nonprofit organizations that benefit children, education, the environment, and fair trade, and has the goal of donating an additional $1 million per year to the BetterWorld Charitable Foundation by 2012. Through its partners Zero Footprint and Trees for the Future, and by way of its own business practices, Kenefick has committed to making BetterWorld Telecom the first carbon-neutral telecommunications carrier in the United States—a goal it achieved in fall 2007. And BetterWorld's list of clients is a who's who of organizations that are making the world a better place, including Patagonia, Greenpeace, Green Mountain Energy, National Peace Corps Association, Honest Tea, Mercy Corps, Enterprise Community Partners, and many others.

James Kenefick has proven that profits and social responsibility can do more than just peacefully coexist—companies that adopt the triple bottom line of people, planet, and profits can *thrive*. Not only that, but James' example is a blueprint for other successful entrepreneurs who would like to do more to give back to their communities—and to make the world a better place for all of us, and for future generations to come. Says James, "It's been a rollercoaster ride, and it hasn't been easy, but now I live every day with a passion for doing good."

Sara Horowitz

Unions have been in decline in the United States for some time now. In the 1950s, 35% of employees belonged to unions. This number shrank to 20% in 1983, and to 12%—or 15.4 million working Americans—in 2006.

Much of these losses can be directly attributed to major layoffs in manufacturing industries—particularly the auto industry. New York-based labor lawyer Sara Horowitz—granddaughter of a former vice president of the International Ladies' Garment Workers' Union—was from her birth steeped in unions, and she had observed firsthand the shift of American jobs from the manufacturing sector to the service sector, particularly to a very fragmented independent workforce of freelancers and other people who worked for themselves, and not for companies. This group is estimated to number some 30 million men and women, including free-lancers, contractors, and temporary workers in the fields of media, technology, domestic child care, and many others.

So, in 1995, Sara created Working Today which—together with another of Sara's creations—the Freelancer's Union—aims to pull together this fragmented population of independent workers and give them a voice, while providing them access to traditional employer-based benefits such as health, life, and disability insurance. According to its website at www.freelancersunion.org, "Freelancers Union is a national nonprofit 501(c)(3) organization that represents the needs and concerns of America's growing independent workforce through advocacy, information and service. Independent workers—freelancers, consultants, independent con-tractors, temps, part-timers, contingent employees and the self-employed—currently make up about 30% of the nation's workforce."

The union exists for three reasons:

- **To enable freelancers to help each other**, whether forming a group to obtain lower rates on insurance, or answering each other's professional questions.
- **To achieve visibility** by working to educate policymakers and the public about the needs of freelancers, advocating for policy changes and—through its surveys—doing research on the independent workforce that no one else is doing.
- **To help freelancers come together** in a nationwide online community to find work and share their knowledge.

Says Sara, "What we're trying to do is create the new institutions that are going to support a new workforce, and to start a broader conversa-tion about how this new economy will work."

Although Freelancer's Union is not very big compared to many long-established union organizations, it is growing. Today, about 16,000 count themselves as members of Freelancer's Union, including 10,000 or so individuals who are receiving health insurance through the organization. And Sara has been rewarded for her efforts to create a self-sustaining organization of flexible workers. She received a John D. and Catherine T. MacArthur Foundation Fellowship in 1999. In 1996, the Stern Family Fund named her a Public Interest Pioneer, and she was also an Echoing Green fellow for four years. Recently she was named as one of *Esquire* magazine's Fifty Best & Brightest.

Despite what she herself has accomplished, Sara doesn't believe you have to be a catalyst for momentous change to have a positive impact on the people and the world around you. Says Sara, "It's funny: I interview a lot of kids who are right out of college, and they always want to be really effective; they really want to change things. I've really grown to like the people who just want to be helpful."

Jim Fruchterman

While you don't have to be a rocket scientist to give back, sometimes it doesn't hurt. This is certainly the case for Jim Fruchterman—former rocket scientist, founder of two highly successful optical character recognition firms, and dedicated social entrepreneur. In 1982, Fruchterman cofounded Calera Recognition Systems, a company that went on to develop optical character recognition software that enabled computers to read almost any piece of printed text. However, Fruchterman soon turned his attention away from the bottom line, and towards solving a persistent social need. In 1989, he founded Arkenstone—a nonprofit social enterprise specializing in the design and production of talking/reading machines for the blind and visually disabled based on the optical character recognition technology developed by Calera Recognition Systems. Since the organization's founding, Arkenstone has delivered talking/reading machines to more than 35,000 disabled people living in 60 countries—in 12 different languages.

But, while this accomplishment might have been the capstone to a remarkably successful career—and the fast track to retirement on a beach somewhere in the South Pacific—Jim Fruchterman wasn't done yet. In 2000, Jim sold Arkenstone and he invested all of the proceeds in a new organization—Benetech—dedicated to using the power of technology to serve humanity. Benetech is a venture capital firm, but one with a difference—it is a nonprofit. The organization specializes in finding, fostering, and financing the development of technology projects addressing major social problems in areas such as disability, human rights, literacy, education, and the digital divide that would typically be ignored by commercial firms because they don't offer a sufficient return on their investment. Says Fruchterman about his job as CEO of Benetech, "I'm an advance scout for social applications. I find exciting technology waiting to be turned into non-commercial tools for disadvantaged groups."

Today, with more than 200 volunteers (most of whom scan and process books for another of his nonprofit ventures—Bookshare.org—which operates under the wing of Benetech), 15 full-time employees, and a plethora of global technology partners, including Sun Microsystems, Hewlett Packard, Sony, IBM, Intel, and many others, Jim Fruchterman and Benetech can point to a long list of accomplishments. This list includes:

- **Route 66 Literacy,** a Web-based program that enables anyone who is literate to help teenagers and adults learn to read and write.
- **Landmine Detection,** by adapting military de-mining tools to safely rid the world of this deadly hazard.
- **Bookshare.org,** for people with vision and reading disabilities, Benetech has created the world's largest accessible digital library of scanned material.
- **Human rights,** by providing science and technology to human rights advocates, strengthening their pursuit of justice and reconciliation.

In addition to the satisfaction that comes from having a positive impact on the world around him, Jim has received no small amount of recognition for his efforts. In 2003 Jim was named an Outstanding Social Entrepreneur by the Schwab Foundation, he received the Robert F. Bray Award from the American Council of the Blind, and he participates in the World Economic Forum in Davos, Switzerland. Jim Fruchterman clearly loves technology, and he knows how to build companies that profit from its application. But, in Jim's mind, that's not enough. Says Fruchterman, "That's our goal, to make sure technology really serves the bigger social issues, rather than just making a buck"

TIPS FOR GIVING BACK

So, let's say you're a CEO, executive, or company owner who wants to give back. Now what? How can you be most effective in your efforts—maximizing your contribution and best leveraging your time, effort, and financial contribution? According to the Washington D.C.-based Institute for Educational Leadership (www.iel.org), there are a number of best practices for business leaders who plan to volunteer to lead community efforts to improve the lives of others:

- **Stay focused.** Identify an area that best suits your interests and abilities—affordable housing or improving workforce skills, for example—and focus on it. Avoid grand, all-encompassing approaches. Don't lose patience if your ideas don't instantly resonate with the people you are trying to help—remember that their previous experiences with "outsiders" may have been dismal.

- **Avoid magic solutions.** Management systems such as total quality management, reengineering, or virtual organizations that work in corporate settings may not work for a government agency or a community. Be practical. Be clear about objectives and expected results.

- **Don't act like a "typical" CEO.** Top-down leadership will not work in community settings. Collaborative and collective leadership are more likely to succeed. Other pointers:
  - You cannot fire people, so don't try.
  - Avoid self-promotion.
  - Respect communities' realities, but make sure that the information you get stands up to tough criteria.
  - Learn to coexist at least temporarily with racial tension while striving to eliminate or reduce it.
  - Try to work within and around restrictive regulations instead of trying to change them, at least at first.

- **Use your best people.** Community activists can easily spot unqualified newcomers. Direct participation from the CEO, a top aide, or any other well-qualified member of the business is best. Whatever the approach, it's important that company representatives have strong, public backing from senior management.

- **Hang in there.** This work isn't easy. Expect the unexpected, because life in poor neighborhoods can be politically messy. Business

leaders working with these communities will encounter problems
of a magnitude and a complexity beyond anything they have dealt
with before. Resist the temptation to bail out when things get
tough. Don't spread yourself too thin, and be flexible.

- **Strive for institutionalization.** Encourage the agency heads and
  community leaders you are working with to think about how to
  make improvements last after you are gone. Once there are promising signs that a reform is taking hold, business volunteers should
  get out of the way and let community members handle
  implementation[5]

In this book, we have strived to inspire you with the examples of men
and women—businesspeople all—who are giving back, and making a
difference in their communities, and in the world around us. Again, there
are many different ways to give back—the best approach is the one that
works best for you. While following the example of others can be a good
way to get started on your path, ultimately, you'll want to tap into your
own passion and follow the path that holds the most meaning for you.

This is the case for each of the leaders that we interviewed and pro-
filed for this book. Each has found a greater purpose in life than simply
making money. While there's nothing wrong with making money, and
the benefit of financial rewards cannot be denied, the men and women
in this book realized that there is more to life, and they took action to
find out exactly what they could do.

It is our sincere hope that you'll join the ranks of the people in this
book, and take the path less traveled—the path of giving back. Perhaps—
like Gary Hirshberg at Stonyfield Farm—you'll take your company along
with you on the journey, transforming it as you yourself are transformed.
Or maybe—like Matt and Jessica Flannery and Kiva.org, you'll create an
entirely new organization with a social mission. Whatever path you
decide to follow, we look forward to reading your story in the not-too-
distant future, and we wish you well on your journey. It won't be easy,
and you'll surely face challenges along the way, but we can guarantee
from our own personal experience that you will feel far more satisfied
and fulfilled by dedicating your life to helping others, and to becoming
an example for others to follow.

NOTES

1. "Companies That Help Gen Y Employees Volunteer Their Workplace Skills to Non-Profits Can Gain Recruiting Advantages, Study Finds," Deloitte & Touche USA press release (April 16, 2007)
2. "Measuring Employee Volunteer Programs: The Human Resources Model," Points of Light Foundation and Center for Corporate Citizenship at Boston College (2005) p.10
3. John Weiser and Simon Zadek, "Conversations with Disbelievers: Persuading Companies to Address Social Challenges," The Ford Foundation (November 2000) p.18
4. "Measuring Employee Volunteer Programs: The Human Resources Model," Points of Light Foundation and Center for Corporate Citizenship at Boston College (2005) p.13
5. "Business Leaders and Communities Working Together for Change," brochure, Institute for Educational Leadership (undated)

Resources for Giving Back

Interested in making a difference in the world around you, but not sure where to start? In the pages that follow, we have collected a variety of websites and blogs that invite you to visit and learn how you can give back, or to learn more about the charities, foundations, and other non-profits that you may be thinking about helping. Along with the name of each site, we include the site's web address, a brief summary of what you'll find when you visit, and a real phone number and mailing address if available. Please understand that websites and blogs come and go, and that this list is current as of November 2007.

CHARITY NAVIGATOR
HTTP://WWW.CHARITYNAVIGATOR.ORG

Charity Navigator—which bills itself as "Your guide to intelligent giving"—is an remarkably comprehensive website for researching and assessing the viability of U.S.-based nonprofit organizations, specifically, charities. According to the site, "Charity Navigator, America's premier independent charity evaluator, works to advance a more efficient and responsive philanthropic marketplace by evaluating the financial health of America's largest charities." And that it does. In 2006, more than four million donors used the Charity Navigator website, which is a two-time *Forbes* award winner for "Best of the Web," was selected by *Reader's Digest* as one of the "100 Best Things about America," and was named by *Esquire* magazine as was one of "41 Ways to Save the World."

Charity Navigator currently rates more than 5,000 nonprofits on a scale of zero to four stars. At the low end of the scale, a rating of zero stars represents an organization that is "Exceptionally Poor—Performs far below industry standards and below nearly all charities in its cause." At the high end of the scale, a rating of four stars representing an organization that is "Exceptional—Exceeds industry standards and outperforms most charities in its cause." In addition to these ratings, Charity Navigator—which is itself a 501(c)(3) organization—presents a variety of useful information, including top-ten lists (such as 10 Best Charities Everyone's Heard Of, and 10 Charities in Deep Financial Trouble), charity CEO compensation studies, tips and resources (including such items as 6 Questions to Ask Charities Before Donating, and Protecting Yourself from Online Scams), and much more.

Charity Navigator
1200 MacArthur Boulevard
Second Floor
Mahwah, New Jersey 07430
201-818-1288
201-818-4694 fax
http://www.charitynavigator.org

GuideStar
http://www.guidestar.org

GuideStar's reason for being is to connect people with nonprofit information, and it accomplishes this by pursuing the following mission: "to revolutionize philanthropy and nonprofit practice by providing information that advances transparency, enables users to make better decisions, and encourages charitable giving." GuideStar encourages nonprofits to share information about their organizations openly and completely. Any nonprofit in the GuideStar database (currently more than 1.7 million organizations) can update its report with information about its mission, programs, leaders, goals, accomplishments, and needs—for free. GuideStar combines the information that nonprofits supply with data from several other sources.

GuideStar is the gold standard when it comes to verifying a nonprofit's legitimacy, learning whether a contribution will be tax deductible, viewing a nonprofit's recent Form 990 (the form required by the IRS to report a nonprofit's annual revenues, expenses, net assets, income-producing activities, program service accomplishments, and more), or finding out more about its mission, programs, and finances. This information can help you make an informed decision when looking for organizations on which to spend your time or money—or both.

GuideStar
4801 Courthouse Street, Suite 220
Williamsburg, VA 23188
757-229-4631
http://www.guidestar.org

Social Venture Partners International
http://www.svpi.org

If you would like to do more in your community than simply write a check for deserving nonprofits, then Social Venture Partners International might be just the ticket. According to the group's Internet home page, Social Venture Partners "is a network of individuals who care passionately about making the world a better place. Fundamental to the Social Venture Partners model is engagement: as well as money, Partners give their time, professional skills, and creativity to work with local nonprofits to meet community needs and bring about positive social change. Social Venture Communities are linked through their membership in the network association, Social Venture Partners International (SVPI)."

Venture Partners share a dual mission. They seek to catalyze significant, long-term positive social change in their communities by:

- Educating individuals to be well informed, effective, and engaged philanthropists;
- Investing time, expertise, and money in innovative nonprofits to strengthen these organizations.

Long story short, you'll find a Social Venture Partner community in many large metropolitan areas of the United States, including Boston, St. Louis, Dallas, Denver, Los Angeles, Portland, Seattle, Charlotte, Minneapolis, Phoenix, and more. As of mid-2007, there are 24 Social Venture Partner organizations and more than 1700 Partners in the USA, Canada, and Japan, who have contributed $23 million in grants to more than 250 nonprofit organizations and countless hours of strategic volunteering contributed to nonprofits.

Social Venture Partners International
1601 Second Avenue, Suite 615
Seattle, WA 98101
206-728-7872
206-728-0552 fax
http://www.svpi.org

KIVA
HTTP://WWW.KIVA.ORG

Kiva—described in detail in Chapter 3 of this book—is the place to go if you would like to make a significant difference in the lives of business-people and entrepreneurs around the world. What's unique—and fun—about Kiva is that you don't simply write a check to the organization and have them decide who is going to get your donation. Via the Kiva web-site, *you* get to decide who gets your money, and how much they get. And one more thing: you're not making a donation when you send money to an entrepreneur via Kiva, you're actually making a loan—a loan that will be repaid by the entrepreneur over time. When your funds are returned, you can loan them to another entrepreneur of your choice.

Kiva is growing like crazy, fueled in great part by extensive media attention. On September 4, 2007, the day Kiva founders Matt Flannery and his wife Jessica appeared on the Oprah Winfrey Show with President Bill Clinton, traffic to the Kiva.org website surged, with 94,000 visits, 4,388 new member signups, and $145,000 in loans raised. On September 5, 2007—the day after their Oprah appearance—Kiva.org experienced 60,000 visits, with 4,067 new member signups and $153,000 in loans raised. In the words of Matt Flannery, "I don't have time to explain the strategy that went into creating this chain of events. Rather, I'll just explain how I feel about it. I'm ecstatic."

Are you ready to fund a business today?

Kiva Microfunds
3180 18th Street, Suite 201
San Francisco, CA 94110
415-641-5482
415-641-1515 fax
http://www.kiva.org

Social Edge
http://www.socialedge.org

Feel like hanging out with a bunch of social entrepreneurs—men and women who are working hard to make the world a better place? Simply point your browser to the Social Edge website, and you'll soon arrive at a place subtitled "by social entrepreneurs, for social entrepreneurs." Sponsored by the Skoll Foundation, Social Edge is a very active global online community where social entrepreneurs and other practitioners of the social benefit sector connect to network, learn, inspire one another—and others—and share resources.

The mission of Social Edge is threefold:

- Connect social entrepreneurs, their partners, and allies to discuss cutting-edge issues shaping the field
- Foster frank dialogue, mutual respect, and a sense of community among all in the sector
- Promote learning from the best, promising, and disastrous practices

Social Edge provides visitors with a variety of interesting things to read and in which to participate, including a number of blogs (some titles: Alyson in Africa, Carter Center, Kiva Chronicles), weekly live discussions (on such topics as Partnerships for Global Solutions, and Changing the World Is Not Enough), and lots of other features and resources. According to the website, Social Edge "has an audience of tens of thousands of social entrepreneurs around the world; it is particularly targeted at social entrepreneurs with limited access to other local resources and practitioners due to the nature of their work (e.g., international development) or their location (e.g., developing countries or in rural areas)."

If you're ready to change the world, then be sure to stop by Social Edge and say "hello" to others who share your dream.

Social Edge/Skoll Fund
250 University Ave #200
Palo Alto, CA 94301
650-331-1031
650-331-1033 fax
http://www.socialedge.org

Idealist
http://www.idealist.org

According to the Idealist.org website, "Idealist is a project of Action Without Borders, a nonprofit organization founded in 1995 with offices in the United States and Argentina. Idealist is an interactive site where people and organizations can exchange resources and ideas, locate opportunities and supporters, and take steps toward building a world where all people can lead free and dignified lives." More specifically, Idealist is a community where visitors can:

- Find: people, organizations, groups, jobs, volunteer opportunities, events, and more
- Sign up: receive daily alerts with new opportunities matching their interests, create a personal profile to network with other Idealists
- Share: invite friends and colleagues to join
- Follow this story: read Idealist's blog, listen to its podcasts, get an RSS feed of any search result on the site
- Post: list their organization on Idealist and post opportunities, program information, events, and more
- Join: find or start an Idealist Group to connect with others

If you're not yet sure what you'd like to do with the rest of your life, Idealist is a great place to browse.

Action Without Borders/Idealist.org
360 West 31st Street, Suite 1510
New York, NY 10001
212-843-3973
212-564-3377 fax
http://www.idealist.org

Net Impact
http://www.netimpact.org

Net Impact is an international nonprofit organization with the mission of making a positive impact on society by growing and strengthening a community of new leaders who use business to improve the world. The organization aims to accomplish this mission by offering a portfolio of programs to educate, equip, and inspire its members (more than 10,000 as of November 2007) to make a tangible difference in their universities, organizations, and communities. Spanning six continents, Net Impact's membership makes up one of the most influential networks of MBAs, graduate students, and professionals in existence today. Net Impact members are current and emerging leaders in corporate social responsibility (CSR), social entrepreneurship, nonprofit management, international development, and environmental sustainability who are actively improving the world.

Networking Opportunities are provided through local chapter events, the annual conference, and online networking tools. Net Impact members consistently rate the organization's network as the most important reason they join and stay involved. In a survey of Net Impact members in early 2007, two-thirds of the respondents reported that they were currently using business to change the world in their graduate school or community, and fully 97 percent said they will use the power of business to improve the world at some point in their career. As one member put it, "I see Net Impact as an opportunity for professionals and students to work together, building the capacity needed to use business as a positive force for change."

Who says businesspeople can't make a difference?

Net Impact
88 First Street, Suite 200
San Francisco, CA 94105
415-495-4230
415-495-4229 fax
http://www.netimpact.org

Social Change Websites
http://socialchangewebsites.com

Wouldn't it be nice if there was one website you could go to find out about lots of other websites dedicated to giving back and changing the world? Actually, there is, and it's name is Social Change Websites. The goal of the organization is "to create a central resource for organizations and causes using the best practices of online advocacy to support their mission." Social Change Websites strives to make this resource as thorough and useful as possible for organizations, volunteers, educators, constituents, and donors.

The website currently catalogs 876 different websites dedicated to social change, arranged by category and state in descending order. Some of these categories include:

- Animal welfare
- Children and youth
- Disability issues
- Faith based
- Health
- Immigration
- Media
- Poverty
- Seniors issues
- Volunteering

All sites are evaluated on content, design quality, usability, and inter-activity. If you're interested in making a difference, Social Change Websites is your one-stop shop for jumpstarting your search for like-minded websites.

http://socialchangewebsites.com

NETWORK FOR GOOD
HTTP://WWW.NETWORKFORGOOD.ORG

If you'd simply like to make a donation to a charity or other nonprofit organization, and you don't want to get caught up in a lot of muss or fuss, then Network for Good might be the ticket for you. According to the site, "Network for Good is the Internet's leading charitable resource, bringing together donors, volunteers and charities online to accomplish good. At www.networkforgood.org, users can donate to more than one million charities and search from among more than 36,000 volunteer opportunities. In addition, non-profits can access tools for fundraising, volunteer recruitment and donor communication. Founded in 2001 by America Online, Cisco Systems and Yahoo!, Network for Good is an independent 501(c) (3) nonprofit organization headquartered in Bethesda, MD."

Since the organization's inception in November 2001, more than 430,000 people have donated more than $100 million to over 20,000 charities through Network for Good. Another 232,555 people have found volunteer opportunities through Network for Good. The organization has also helped more than 6,000 nonprofits raise funds, cultivate donors and recruit volunteers through its online tools.

If you decide to do more than donate, Network for Good has an excellent volunteer opportunity search tool. Simply fill in your area of interest, your zip code, and any keywords you like, and you'll be presented with a list of possibilities.

Network for Good
7920 Norfolk Avenue, Suite 520
Bethesda, MD 20814
866-650-4636
240-482-3215 fax
http://www.networkforgood.org

VOLUNTEERMATCH
HTTP://WWW.VOLUNTEERMATCH.ORG

If you're still looking for an opportunity to give back by volunteering, but haven't yet found the situation that's right for you, then give VolunteerMatch a chance to go to work on your behalf. VolunteerMatch is the leading online organization dedicated to helping people find a great place to volunteer. The organization accomplishes this goal by offering a variety of online services to support a community of nonprofit, volunteer and business leaders committed to civic engagement. VolunteerMatch's popular service welcomes millions of visitors a year (4.7 million in 2006) and has become the preferred Internet recruiting tool for more than 40,000 nonprofit organizations, including such organizations as American Red Cross, National Multiple Sclerosis Society, MATHCOUNTS, Habitat for Humanity, Keep America Beautiful, Senior Corps, and many others.

VolunteerMatch also specializes in helping companies (including Merrill Lynch, Johnson & Johnson, Merck, Gap, Target, Google, Dell, and many others) set up their own employee volunteer programs, using the VolunteerMatch website as a portal. According to research cited on the site, "companies that help employees volunteer with nonprofit organizations could have a leg up with recruiting Generation Y (18–26 year-old) talent. Nearly two-thirds of the respondents (62 percent) in the 2007 Volunteer IMPACT survey by Deloitte & Touche USA said they would prefer to work for companies that give them opportunities to contribute their talents to nonprofit organizations."

Ready? Set. Volunteer!

VolunteerMatch
717 California St., Second Floor
San Francisco, CA 94108
(415) 241-6868
(415) 241-6869 fax
http://www.volunteermatch.org

Change.org
http://www.change.org

Though still a lightweight in its impact on the world—having collected donations of only about $50,000 since its launch in February 2007—Change.org is poised to be the next big thing in giving. The site—a social network for social activism, incorporating nonprofits, politicians, and people across the globe—has attracted lots of media attention and more than 31,000 people have signed on as members. According to the site, "To augment the power of the grassroots networks that develop through Change.org, we help connect these networks to the many non-profit organizations that are already working to advance worthy causes around the world—over 1 million in total. We facilitate dialogue and collaboration by creating a social network around each nonprofit, thereby allowing people to participate in ways never before possible—by posting ideas and suggestions, engaging in direct dialogue, and organizing communities of donors, volunteer events, and rallies."

Visitors to the Change.org site can join with others in "virtual foundations," focused on addressing a wide variety of social needs, including child abuse, Darfur, poverty, sustainable development, and much more. The site also allows members to organize around political candidates, including current presidential candidates Rudy Giuliani, Barack Obama, Ron Paul, Mitt Romney, Hillary Clinton, and others. When asked how the site makes the money it needs to fund its operations, founder Ben Rattray says, "We take 1 percent of all donations, and we charge for premium services to nonprofits that allow them to brand their network and add additional features to their community."

http://www.change.org

FUTURE LEADERS IN PHILANTHROPY
HTTP://FLIP.ONPHILANTHROPY.COM

To understand what the Future Leaders in Philanthropy (FLiP) believes in, you need look no further than the home page of its website/blog, which declares: "We are the future leaders in philanthropy. By working together, we will further our careers, serve our organizations' mission, and change the world. FLiP is dedicated to creating a community and a network where other future leaders can meet, learn, exchange ideas, and contribute to each other's success." If you're new to the idea of giving back, or if you'd like to network with like-minded men and women, then the FLiP site is a good place to aim your browser.

Recent posts include "Craig Newmark gives web advice for small nonprofits," "Meet-A-FLiP: Elizabeth R. Miller," "Craigslist Boot Camp 2007," and "A new conversation for change." Ready to change the world? Get set—go!

Future Leaders in Philanthropy: FLiP
http://flip.onphilanthropy.com

TACTICAL PHILANTHROPY
HTTP://WWW.TACTICALPHILANTHROPY.COM

Tactical Philanthropy is a thought-provoking blog run by prolific writer and financial advisor Sean Stannard-Stockton. Sean is a principal and director of Tactical Philanthropy at Ensemble Capital Management in Burlingame, CA. Ensemble Capital provides families both traditional investment management and a unique, specialized approach to advancing their philanthropic interests. He writes the column On Philanthropy which appears monthly in the Wealth at the Weekend section of the *Financial Times* and he is author of the chapter "The Evolution of the Tactical Philanthropist" in the anthology *Mapping the New World of American Philanthropy*.

According to Stannard-Stockton, "To practice Tactical Philanthropy is to organize, optimize, and transfer philanthropic capital in ways that maximize the impact of the donor's strategic plan. It is the practice of transforming philanthropic strategy into reality."

Recent posts include such topics as "Charitable Bankers, Total Strategists, Britney Spears & Kevin Smith," "Extreme Philanthropy," "The Giving Carnival," and "Evaluating High-Impact Nonprofits." You'll also find a variety of podcast interviews on the Tactical Philanthropy site, including:

- Interview with Cheryl Dahle, employee number 24 at *Fast Company* magazine, responsible for the launch of the Fast Company Social Capitalist Awards.
- Interview with Stacy Palmer, editor of the *Chronicle of Philanthropy*. Stacy was involved in founding the paper in 1988, the leading newspaper in the philanthropic sector.
- Interview with Paul Shoemaker, founding president of Social Venture Partners, who defends the venture capital concept and criticizes "big mouthed," arrogant individuals for diluting the term "venture philanthropy."

http://www.tacticalphilanthropy.com

1Year1Book—4Free
http://www.booksforfree.org

Inspired by the men and women that he and Bert Berkley interviewed for this book, Peter Economy decided to embark on a new project: 1Year1Book—4 Free. Late one night Peter was wondering: "What could I do that would really make a difference—more than just writing a check, or contributing an hour or two here or there?" The idea came to him in a flash: He could write a book for someone who had a great idea, but who was outside of the publishing industry and needed some help getting their foot in the door.

However, the more he thought about it, Peter realized that there was an even better idea—an idea that would allow him to give back in a way that would best tap his creativity and passion for writing: Starting in 2008, Peter has committed to help make the world a better place by writing one book a year—for free, from now until he can no longer write—with all the proceeds (advance and royalties) going to a 501(c)(3) nonprofit organization of his selected coauthor's choice. Peter hopes that he'll help create at least 30 free books over the next several decades.

So . . . if you've ever wanted to write a book, and if you've got a great idea, and you'd like to help change the world by giving all the proceeds to a nonprofit of your choice, then be sure to visit www.booksforfree .org and submit a one-page pitch for consideration by Peter's three-member panel of judges (comprised of Frances Hesselbein, former CEO of Girl Scouts USA; James Phills, director of the Stanford Center for Social Innovation; and Mick Ukleja, founder and president of LeadershipTraQ).

Someone *will* be chosen each year—why not you?

1Year1Book—4Free
Peter Economy
P.O. Box 611
La Jolla, CA 92038
619-566-5554
http://www.booksforfree.org

Index